Watering Hole

The Colorful History of Booze, Sex & Death at a New Jersey Tavern

By

Matt Connor

This book is a work of non-fiction. Names and places have been changed to protect the privacy of all individuals. The events and situations are true.

ISBN: 1-4107-8017-1 (e-book)
ISBN: 1-4140-0303-X (Paperback)

This book is printed on acid free paper.

1stBooks - rev. 09/08/03

Dedicated to the memory of four friends
who by their passing leave a sad void in my life.

Dr. Saundra Hybels
Sybil Carlin
Rosemary Clooney
Evelyn Lane

CONTENTS

PRELUDE TO PART I

When young Davey Moore stepped into the tavern at the Cox Hotel that cold Thanksgiving evening, he had no way of knowing that his life was about to change forever. For Davey, the night was to be spent in a typically unsupervised fashion, running around with his pals while his mother and father got drunk at a local boarding house or in their own two-room home in a miner's shantytown a short distance from the hotel. Though the iron mines that employed Davey's father were closed for Thanksgiving, on this most American of holidays the Moore household was unlikely to have been the scene of much feasting or celebration.

Davey's parents, Solomon David (known simply as Dave) and Mary Ann Moore were both Irish immigrants who eked out a meager living on Dave's miner's wages. Married in Ireland and residents of Mine Hill for about ten years, Dave and Mary Ann fought regularly for any number or reasons, among them religion (Dave was protestant, or "Orange" in the parlance of the time; Mary Ann was a Catholic, or "Green"), politics and Mary Ann's chores around the house. These arguments often led to physical confrontations that would leave Mary Ann bruised and bleeding.

Dave was a few years Mary Ann's senior, with light hair, small, quick eyes and a wide mouth with thin lips. She was fair-haired and stout but frail, and previous beatings at the hands of her husband had injured her to such an extent that she could walk only with the assistance of a cane.

Young Davey spent many nights away from home, engaging in various boyhood adventures with his friends. Though he would later say that he was unafraid of his father, and that these nights spent away from home were unrelated to the violence in the household, one could easily understand why the young man would want to steer clear of his parents during their drinking sprees.

As parents, Dave and Mary Ann Moore were inattentive at best and negligent at worst, at least by today's standards. Indeed, much of the time they would have had no idea where Davey was or what he was up to. He rarely attended school and could barely read. In fact, if anyone had asked him how old he was, he couldn't have given a straight answer. He might have been twelve or he might have been fifteen, he truly had no idea. But he was bright and intelligent and in this small town of a few hundred souls he was fairly well known.

At the Cox Hotel Davey likely encountered James Cox, the hotel's proprietor. If there was a state-mandated drinking age at the time, it was largely unenforced and James would have paid it little heed. Despite his obviously tender years, if young Davey had plunked down a few cents for some Jersey Lightning—the potent, apple-derived intoxicant so popular at the time—James probably would have served some up for the boy.

One can imagine James and Davey having a brief conversation over the brew. They might have talked baseball. Thirty-two year old James Cox was the oldest of four brothers and two of the Cox boys had been members of the local team. Or they might have talked about recent mining accidents, as fatalities at the mines were so commonplace at the 22 iron mining locations scattered throughout town that barely a fortnight went by without news of further loss of life. Or they might have talked about that dreadful incident over in Dover just three weeks previous, when an Italian immigrant named Luigi Lusignani arrived in town to pick up his wife, Johanna Moosi, who was living with another man. The papers said Johanna was "a fallen woman," a practicing "woman of the Town" and her naive young husband wanted to take her back to New York City, where they had met and wed just a few months prior. But things turned sour and Luigi stabbed Johanna to death in broad daylight on the front porch of a shoe store on the corner of Blackwell and Warren streets.

James and Davey could have chatted about all of these things, or they might not have talked about any of them. Davey remained at the Cox Hotel for an indeterminate amount of time. He had left home around 6:30 p.m., at about the same time that his parents were receiving a visitor, Tom Madden, a miner in his twenties (later described as "a lusty, vigorous daredevil fellow, and given to license") who had spent the holiday drinking at Terrence Connelly's, a local unlicensed bar and boarding house also popular with Davey's parents.

Before leaving home, Davey told his mother that he was going out with some other boys, and Mary Ann told him that Tom Madden was going to stop by. Davey could tell that his mother was already intoxicated. As he stepped out the front door, Davey saw Madden approaching their home, also obviously intoxicated. Davey told his father that Madden was coming, and a short time later young Davey was on his way to the Cox Hotel.

Davey spent the rest of the night running around with his pals. After leaving the hotel, he went to a store in town, perhaps the shop owned by Joseph Harvey across the street from the Cox Hotel. He spent a good deal of time at Connelly's, that same unlicensed bar and boarding house at which his parents and Tom Madden were regulars. Davey was friendly with the Connellys' son, James, and he often spent the night at James' house. He also spent part of the night sleeping in a hay wagon.

By noon the following day, Davey would be in police custody, his father would be on the run from the law, and the semi-nude and partially-frozen body of his mother would be found beaten to death near a brook behind his home.

Early on Friday morning, November 29th, the day after Thanksgiving, Tom Madden took a little "hair of the dog." Then he took a little more. He had passed out on the Moore's kitchen floor the previous evening and, he would later relate, his mother had come after a time and taken him home to bed. But his long bender continued almost as soon as he opened his eyes the next day. By noon he had already consumed a quart of liquor he had purchased from a Mrs. McGary, then went to Connelly's and bought a half-gallon of beer, which he promptly drank. Then on to the tavern at the Cox Hotel, where he put a couple of drinks away before heading to an uncle's home for about a week.

When Tom Madden left the Cox Hotel that afternoon, James Cox would have had no way of knowing that the man to whom he had just served drinks would, within days, have an accusation of battery and rape lodged against him.

Neither would Cox have known that Madden's name would soon appear in newspapers across the Northeastern United States in connection with one of the most brutal murders to occur in the history of the state of New Jersey.

No, he had no way of knowing any of this. But he was about to find out.

PART ONE
1861-1961

CHAPTER ONE

Stagecoach days

Call them bar keeps, tavern proprietors or saloonkeepers. By whatever name, they're easily among the most popular—and sometimes notorious—residents of any small town, for obvious reasons. They supply the liquor that fuels celebrations, lend a sympathetic ear to the down-on-their luck, break up fights and—when necessary—toss out the nuisance inebriate who's spoiling everyone's good time. But the saloonkeeper's fame is often fleeting compared with that of local clergymen and political figures, whose names live on in church records, minutes of town meetings, local histories, monuments, plaques and newspaper stories.

A generation or two after the saloon keeper leaves town or dies, he or she may be completely forgotten by all but his or her closest friends and relatives. And like most private citizens, the evidence that these individuals ever walked the face of the earth may exist only in a few scant documents buried in municipal archives, or on the face of a grave marker.

This simple fact makes it difficult to know much about the lives of the men and women who built and operated the Mine Hill Hotel through the early years of its existence. Located in Morris County's Mine Hill, the hotel has in recent years been converted to a restaurant. It is situated at the intersection of what was once referred to simply as "the road from Crane's Corner to the Dickerson Mine" (now West Randolph Ave.) and "the road to Dover" (now Randolph Ave.). It lies in what is commonly known as the "Irishtown" section of the village, named for the predominantly Irish immigrants who resided in a collection of dwellings located between what is now Randolph Ave. and Jackson's Brook, built by the mining companies to house their laborers and sometimes their families.

With a basic structural design that closely resembles many other hotels and taverns of New Jersey's mid-19th century, the former Mine Hill Hotel is a three-story structure, with its ground floor serving as a tavern and dining area. The second floor was accessible by an exterior railed walkway, which would have been ideal for unloading guest luggage onto the roofs of waiting stagecoaches. This floor housed "hotel" rooms, though the rooms contained few of the modern conveniences we associate with hotel/motel accommodations today. Essentially a boarding house, the property would have offered sparsely furnished rooms with a pot-bellied stove, bed, and perhaps a wash basin. There was no electricity or running water in the establishment for decades, and even as late as 1960, customers were obliged to use outdoor facilities when nature called. The third floor of the property was used as housing for owners and managers.

There is a strong oral tradition that the hotel began as a stagecoach stop; a notion embraced for decades because of the romance and sepia-toned nostalgia it inspires. But because some long-time (and well-meaning) residents had a tendency to embellish local history, there are others in town who rightly question the validity of some longtime assumptions about the property. For example, the idea that the Mine Hill Hotel was built over 200 years ago, in the late 1700s or early 1800s, is inaccurate. Despite previously published statements about the age of the property, deed records and maps of the area confirm that the establishment was built around 1868.

Just the same, the property was almost certainly was a stop on a stagecoach route, though documentary verification is extremely difficult to come by. Private companies with lax regulation operated stagecoaches. When the last of these companies had gone out of business after the turn of the twentieth century, there was little reason to preserve the company records, which may have described specific routes and the stops along the way. State laws regarding stagecoach operations were not so specific as to dictate when and where the stages stopped or what their origins and destinations were.

Still, there is strong circumstantial evidence to indicate that the popular horse-drawn carriages paused regularly at the entrance of the Mine Hill Hotel to pick up and drop off passengers. Perhaps the most obvious evidence of its stagecoach stop origins is the fact that hotels are developed to accommodate travelers, so they are placed at locations through which travelers are most likely to pass. Today hotels are found surrounding airports and bus depots and on major highways. In the 18th and 19th centuries they were built along stagecoach routes. At the time the Mine Hill Hotel was built, people traveled long distances over land either by stagecoach or by rail, so it simply makes logical sense that this particular hotel was built at a location where stages would have stopped.

Jack E. Bouscher, in his history of Atlantic County, NJ, "Absegami Yesteryear" wrote about early transportation in southern New Jersey in some detail. A few of his observations are applicable to the origins of the Mine Hill Hotel, given its location at the intersection of two main roads through town, the "road from Crane's Corner to the Dickerson Mine" and the "road to Dover."

Bouscher wrote that "a stage, speeding sometimes as fast as ten miles an hour behind a team of pounding horses, invariably generated dense clouds of stifling dust, which settled on driver, riders and cargo. Small wonder, then, the inns and taverns of the day, *spotted at nearly every crossroad*, did a thriving business in ale and applejack" (emphasis added).

Other works provide revealing details into the appearance and operation of taverns and inns of the northern section of the state. In his book, "Life in Early New Jersey," Harry B. Weiss wrote that during the late eighteenth century—admittedly a period that predates the construction of the Mine Hill Hotel—"the taverns in the north of New Jersey were generally of two classes, one for the accommodation of stagecoach and private travelers, and one where teamsters and drivers 'put up.'" Further, he wrote, "As the villages increased in size in the nineteenth century, country hotels sprang up for use of commercial travelers. These places had rooms on the second floor, frequently unheated in winter, a bar in which there was a big stove and some chairs, and an old-fashioned desk on which reposed the hotel register. Behind the desk was a wooden board on which the room keys hung. This type of small-town hotel was found everywhere, even into the twentieth century. They were patronized by commercial travelers, and the bars catered to them as well as to the townspeople. The customers did not expect much in the way of comfort, although in some places the food was excellent. There were stables and sheds for horses, too."

Weiss could have been describing the Mine Hill Hotel in its early days, so close is his description to what is known of the property in its late 1800s period.

The peak time for stagecoach travel in New Jersey was 1800 to 1835, at which point rail service began to cut deeply into established stagecoach routes. Still, coaches continued to travel New Jersey's roadways until just after 1900, and horse-drawn transportation continued at least through the teen years of the twentieth century, when the popularity of the Ford Motor Company's Model T initiated the automobile's rise to dominance in land travel.

Not coincidentally, the glory days of stagecoaches paralleled the "turnpike era" of Garden State transportation, when massive road building projects connected far-flung areas of the state for the first time. The construction of these roads would greatly improve the progress of stagecoaches. The first of many toll roads chartered by the state to link previously inaccessible areas of New Jersey was the Morris Turnpike. In 1801, according to Wheaton J. Lane's landmark 1939 book, "From Indian Trail to Iron Horse: Travel and Transportation in New Jersey, 1620-1860" the Morris Turnpike was built and financed in three sections. The first ran from Elizabeth through Springfield and Chatham to Morristown; the second through Succasunna (on Mine Hill's southeastern border) to Stanhope; the third to Newton. Later a road between Morristown and Easton, called the "Washington Turnpike," became tremendously popular. Mail stages passed daily between Elizabeth and Easton, Pennsylvania and, Lane wrote, "as early as 1810 Schooley's Mountain [in Long Valley] attracted summer vactionists because of its favorable location and excellent spring water."

In Mine Hill, there are at least two theories regarding possible stage routes through town, one of which fits neatly into the descriptions of the turnpike/stagecoach routes above. Lifelong resident Ken Ebner related this theory to Elaine Campoli, the former president of the local historical society. In May of 1998, 81-year-old Ebner said that Art Glass (whose family had owned the Mine Hill Hotel for fifty years beginning in 1911) and lifelong Morris County resident Pauline O'Brien-Wagner had told him that the stagecoach route started in Newark, and upon arrival in Mount Fern (just east of Mine Hill) the stage driver would blow his horn to alert the folks at the Mine Hill Hotel that the coach was on the way. The coach would then proceed down the remaining portion of West Randolph Ave. to Canfield Ave.; then on to the Sussex Turnpike, which was then a toll road; the coach would then continue on to Route 10; to Route 24; and stop at the mineral springs for water at Schooley's Mountain. From there the coach would proceed to Easton for a few days.

Other sources echo some of the more colorful details of Ebner's account, such as the coachman who would blow his horn prior to making a stop. George Quarrie, for example, wrote in his book "Within A Jersey Circle" of the excitement of hearing an approaching stagecoach on what was possibly the most well-traveled stage route of all, the Old York Road.

"Thus came the great chariot, tearing down the street of the town or village, behind the magnificent, foaming horses, spurred on by a blast of the bugle. The crash of the wheels of the towering equipage, the splendid connecting link between the two great cities of New York and Philadelphia, was inspiring and electrifying to everybody."

Despite the folksiness and detail of Ebner's account, however, there are a few problems with his story. For one thing, by the time the Mine Hill Hotel was built, the Morris & Essex Railroad was regularly carrying passengers—faster, and at cheaper rates—between Newark and Morristown and on to Dover, which lies on Mine Hill's northeastern border. In Morristown there was a connection to the Lehigh Valley Express train to Easton, making the stagecoach journey, at that time, practically irrelevant.

Ebner died prior to the writing of this book, but his younger brother Albert "Abbie" Ebner cautioned that Ken had a way of embellishing his tales of Mine Hill's past. Told of his brother's account of the stagecoach route through town, Abbie said, "There's no one to prove him wrong, nor is there any reason to embarrass his memory by challenging the credibility of his story, but Ken was noted for creating his own version of Mine Hill's colorful history."

For one thing, Abbie Ebner said, his brother was a non-drinker, and therefore would have had little occasion to speak with Art Glass, who spent most of his time behind the bar of his little tavern. He added, however, that he himself believed strongly that the Mine Hill Hotel was indeed a stagecoach stop at one time. Unfortunately he didn't have evidence to back up this statement.

A more likely scenario than the one Ken Ebner described is that the Mine Hill Hotel served as a stop on a short route between Dover and Succasunna, an 8.5 mile span. This theory was posed by—

7

among others—Robert Wolff, who with local historian Allison Jost began compiling historical data on the town in 1975.

After the establishment of the railroads in the 1830s, stagecoaches survived by providing transportation between train stations and the towns not serviced directly by railroads. The local newspapers all ran railroad schedules, and with them information on connecting stage lines. One of these stage lines ran to Succasunna, Flanders and Hackettstown on the arrival of the a.m. and p.m. trains at Dover. Since the main roads from Dover to Succasunna at the time would have taken the stagecoach directly past the Mine Hill Hotel, it makes sense that the hotel would have been a convenient place to stop.

So what was stagecoach travel like during the early years of the operation of the Mine Hill Hotel? Though colonial stagecoach travel was, according to Walter Van Hoesen's "Early Taverns and Stagecoach Days in New Jersey," a "wearying, bone-jarring" experience, later, in the 19th century, stagecoaches adopted metal springs on their axles to provide for a more comfortable ride.

"As competition among stage lines became greater, such luxuries as straw-filled cushions for the hard board seats were added," wrote James and Margaret Cawley in their book "Along the Old York Road." "However, none of those early stage wagons could be described as comfortable to any degree."

Further, the Cawleys wrote, "Most of the stage drivers were arrogant and couldn't care less about the comfort of their passengers. To hold to their schedules was the main consideration and whether the customers were jolted unmercifully apparently was no concern of the driver. Doubtless the increased competition for business later changed that attitude to some degree."

The discomfort suffered by the passengers was broken up by frequent and refreshing stops along the way, however. Cornelius Vermeule wrote about this in his article, "Early Transportation in and About New Jersey" (*Proceedings of the New Jersey Historical Society, series IX*).

"People were then conservative," Vermeule wrote. "They had never before traveled thirty miles without eating, or ten without drinking. They had been accustomed to exchanging views and compliments, and gathering the latest news and gossip at each tavern where horses were changed. Racing across open country at 20 miles per hour was well enough, but to pass such places as New Brunswick, with Rutgers College, or the State Capital, without having a word with their friends was unthinkable. Traveling to them was not simply transportation. It meant pleasures which they were loath to forgo."

As with other properties like it across the state, the stagecoach stop/tavern in Mine Hill was likely a hub of community activity. Indeed, little of what went on in the little town would have escaped the notice of the habitues of the local tavern, where news, gossip and tall tales would have been freely exchanged. In all likelihood, the tavern would have been the first place a newcomer might have gone to find out which of the mines were hiring. It would have been the place to find out how the sports teams were doing in Dover, Boonton or Port Oram. And when a crime was committed in the area, the local tavern would have been the first place folks would have congregated to find out the latest information.

In 1967, Thomas Taber also wrote about stagecoach travel, specifically in Morris County, for the New Jersey Historical Society. And in his account, the drivers were considerably less surly—and considerably more inebriated—than those described by the Cawleys.

"Stops were frequent to rest, water, or change horses," Taber wrote, "and as they were made at public houses, passengers had plenty of time to stretch their legs, and to fortify themselves with a few shots of good 'Jersey Lightening' to sustain them until the next stop. As it was customary for the passengers to invite the jolly, ever-willing driver 'to have a little something' at each stop, there were occasions when the stagecoach arrived at its final destination with only the exhausted, hard-driven horses being sober."

Even the turnpike tollgates would have been considered unbelievably quaint by today's standards. Typically they were long poles extended low across the road, with a family residing in a nearby "toll house" responsible for collecting the money from passing coaches. When the toll was paid, the pole was raised to allow the coach to pass through. As late as 1915 a few of these old-style tollgates were still in operation in New Jersey.

In 1923, the *Newark Evening News* took a look back at the old stagecoach days, pointing out that older residents of Sussex borough remembered well the days when stages still ran through the area:

"when the stage driver, a picturesque old fellow that he was, brought his four horses into town at a flying canter with the stage coach rocking perilously behind, halted them with a flourish in front of the hotel, flung the reins to an attendant and put up for the night."

This *Evening News* story concluded on the note that the days of stage coach drivers is dead, that they had been "doomed when the 'new fangled' steam engine raced the old white horse and won. But his place is in history, for it was through his hardihood and grit that communication in those early days was maintained and progress made possible."

CHAPTER TWO

Miner considerations

The Mine Hill Hotel had not yet been erected when Randolph Township resident John M. Yatman (sometimes spelled Yetman) and his wife, Amelia, owned the property on the corner of "the road from Crane's Corner to the Dickerson Mine" and "the road to Dover." Prior to 1861—the year they sold this property to Henry C. Byram—the land where the Mine Hill Hotel would one-day stand was just a plot on the Yatman farm.

Byram was also a resident of Randolph (Mine Hill was at that time a section of Randolph, from which it seceded in 1923) when Yatman sold the property to him, for $3,500. Old documents like the Yatman-Byram deed are notoriously difficult to comprehend, as they were written in cursive long hand (with grammatical and spelling liberties taken along the way) and old-style legalese, with much surveyor's jargon thrown in. Land measurements, for example, were taken in "chains" and "links," so that the Yatman property is described as "Beginning at the most westerly corner of a tract of land belonging to Barnabus Horton etc. and Joseph C. Harvey's line thence coming (1) south sixty five degrees west ten chains and sixty links to the corner of John Byram's land in the said Harvey's line…"

Other survey references commonly named landmarks like "a large chestnut tree," "a large rock in the brook," or a "post in the ground," as boundary indicators. This makes it nearly impossible to trace specific locations 145 years later, when the territory surrounding a property was likely to have been substantially altered.

It should be pointed out that the John Byram mentioned in the above deed reference was the father of purchaser Henry C. Byram, and a figure of some historical significance in New Jersey.

Yatman himself was about 40, and had substantial land holdings in 1861. He and his wife, Amelia, had three children, a boy and two girls. A year and a half after he sold the property to Henry Byram, Yatman was enrolled in the Union army in the Civil War as a private. He was mustered in on September 19, 1862 and served nine months with Company G of the Twenty-Seventh New Jersey

Regiment. That regiment was organized in Camp Frelinghuysen in Newark and was in reserve in the first Battle of Fredricksburg, a defeat for the Union troops that led, in part, to the replacement of General Ambrose Burnside with Major General Joseph Hooker in January, 1863.

According to "A History of Randolph Township, Morris County, NJ," the morale of the troops in which Yatman served was "reportedly high" when they were mustered out in Newark in July of 1863: "each man would probably have taken a position along with other New Jersey troops at Gettysburg had they been employed." The regiment was unharmed by Confederate gunfire, and more suffered from diseases such as diarrhea and typhoid than from other battlefield hazards.

A bit more is known about Henry Conklin Byram, who bought the land from Yatman in 1861. The son of John Byram, Henry purchased several other tracts of land from his father in the summer of 1861, four months after buying the Yatman land. The Byrams were an important Morris County family, having been descended from blueblood Byrams who first arrived on American shores via the Mayflower. General George Washington was said to have camped at a Byram family farm during the Revolutionary War, and Byram Township, NJ, was named after one of Henry Byram's ancestors.

Besides being owner of huge chunks of Mine Hill land (an entire stretch of Randolph Ave.—encompassing as many as fifteen miner's houses—was known as "Byram Row"), John Byram was the proprietor of the Byram Iron Mine, which was the first mine in the state to utilize a steam engine in its operations, thus making it, however briefly, the most technologically-advanced mining operation in the state. Over it's forty years of operation, the Byram Mine produced an estimated 600,000 tons of ore, second among its contemporaries only to the nearby Dickerson Mine, which was operated for a far longer period of time.

The land-holdings and mine operations made the Byrams quite wealthy, and in 1860 Henry C. Byram was among the richest men in Randolph Township, with land and other assets valued at $23,000— equal to more than $457,000 today—a fortune at a time when the typical miner was lucky to be making $400 a year.

It would be impossible to write about the history of the Mine Hill Hotel without talking about the history of iron mines and its industry in New Jersey. Mine Hill took its name from the mining industry, and as many as 22 iron mines were operated in the three-square-mile village between 1713 and 1966, when Scrub Oaks, the last iron mine in the state, closed its doors. Mahlon Dickerson—Mine Hill's most famous historic figure—began managing the oldest and most productive mine in the state, the Dickerson Mine, in 1807. It had been acquired previously by his father, Jonathon Dickerson, in 1780 and run as the Succasunny Iron Mining Company. During its 175-plus years of operation, over one million tons of ore was extracted from the Dickerson Mine, some of which was said to have been used to build muskets and ammunition for Washington's army during the Revolutionary War.

Mine owner Mahlon Dickerson also served in the U.S. Senate, the New Jersey Legislature, New Jersey Supreme Court, and was governor of New Jersey (1813-15) and Secretary of the Navy under Presidents Andrew Jackson and Martin Van Buren. His vast estate, "Ferromonte," was built with the enormous wealth the Dickerson Mine earned him. Demolished in 1965, the estate—with its gardens full of exotic plants and mansion with its library full of rare books—was located just off of what is now Canfield Ave. in Mine Hill, less than one mile around the bend from where the former Mine Hill Hotel now stands.

Because the Mine Hill Hotel property was located directly along the route that the mine workers—mostly Irish immigrants—would have traversed on their way to and from the Dickerson Mine to their homes in Irishtown, it can be assumed the property's fortunes would have risen and fallen with the success of the local mining industry. As the only licensed tavern in Irishtown, the Mine Hill Hotel's tavern was characterized as a "miner's bar" from its first day of operation through the closure of the last mine in the state.

The tavern's clientele was therefore made up largely of rugged, hard-bitten men who daily risked life and limb under the most hazardous conditions. When the miners held a strike (as they did occasionally between 1867 and 1894), there surely would have been discussion and argument at the tavern over the labor situation. When mine accidents occurred, they undoubtedly would have been a topic of heated conversation at the tavern. With virtually no safety precautions taken against the risk of cave-ins or other accidents, accounts of mine injuries and fatalities appear frequently in local papers of the late 1800s. The following excerpts from the Morris County *Jerseyman* and *Dover Iron-Era* newspapers paint a clear but frightening picture of life in the mines:

APRIL 19, 1879: "On Saturday night of last week, as Michael Gannon was descending the mine at Randall Hill, he accidently missed his hold on the ladder, and fell to the bottom of the mine, the distance being about fifty feet. After nearly an hour had passed, he was discovered by the men in an insensible state, and carried to his residence."

FEBRUARY 19, 1881: "On Monday morning early, an accident occurred at the Dickerson Mine that has since confined Mr. W. Pearce to his bed in very critical condition. It seems in going down the ladder he missed his hold and fell a perpendicular distance of about forty feet, then striking the shaft, he fell the remaining fifty feet to the bottom. Strange to say, when found he was not insensible. Drs. King and Richie have been attending him and as yet his condition is uncertain."

APRIL 15, 1881: "James Meagher, at the Baker Mine, Mine Hill, met with a terrible death last Monday night while descending one of the new shafts. His brother was just below him and he was either in the act of getting upon a ladder or was within a few rounds of the top when from some course, probably slipping, he lost his hold and plunged down the shaft…"

JULY 7, 1881: "Friday night of last week three young men were injured in the Byram Mine while engaged in drilling out a blast hole that had failed to explode…"

JULY 29, 1881: "David Miller, a boss of the night shift in the Baker Mine, was killed Tuesday night by a large mass of iron ore falling on him. He was unmarried and was the sole support of his mother. He was about 35 years old."

MARCH 20, 1885: "The Dickerson Mine, at Mine Hill, commenced to cave in last Friday and at last accounts had not ceased. The damage is in the main shaft and the mass already fallen is enormous. It happened at a very fortunate time, as the one shift of men had come up and the other had not gone down yet..."

AUGUST 7, 1885: "A very serious 'cave' occurred at the Dickerson Mine last week. The pillar which supported the collar of the cowbelly shaft collapsed and in its fall carried away a portion of the horse railroad track, the summit slope of the old mine, landing brace of cowbelly pump roads, oscillating bob, wire rope &c. Fortunately it happened during the midnight supper hour, so that I have not to chronicle any loss of life. About twenty men were thrown out of work."

JULY 4, 1890: "Patrick Carbey, a machinist at the Baker Mine, Mine Hill, was engaged in fixing a pulley rope last Saturday when he fell from the pulley platform and went down about 25 feet. He struck in a sitting posture and so affected his spine that his extremities were paralyzed."

An early account of iron mining in the area was published in *Harper's New Monthly Magazine* in an April, 1860 article entitled "An Artist-Life in the Highlands." In this piece, author-illustrators John Chapin, J.W. Orr (dubbed "Neutral Tint" for the purposes of the article) and his brother Nathaniel Orr (dubbed "Snell") take a stagecoach from Paterson to Newfoundland, have several adventures and end their travels in Mine Hill, where they visit the Dickerson and Byram Mines. In Dover they meet Henry Conklin Byram, who was in his late 30s at the time and who offers to give the *Harper's* staffers a tour of his father's mine in Mine Hill.

The journalists mention "a beautiful 40-horse power [steam] engine" under construction at the time. After a walk around the grounds of the mine complex, Henry, the authors state, "seemed to be at some pains to point out several disabled and smashed up cars, the results of the accidental breaking of chains, by which they had been allowed to descend to the bottom of the slope [of one shaft of the

Byram Mine] with tremendous force, in one instance resulting in the death of two miners who were unfortunately in their way."

The *Harper's* writer/illustrators were then cajoled by Henry to climb into one of the mineshaft cars and travel all the way to the bottom, a journey at times thrilling and harrowing: "They were again startled out of their propriety, when, having descended about 150 feet, the bottom of the car leaped up very suddenly from the track, and struck the wall above them with a bump which threw Snell back upon his companion and upset the latter out upon the track. They were restored to equanimity by the uproarious laughter which greeted their accident; and as soon as they could pick themselves up, and their eyes became accustomed to the gloom, they discovered that they had arrived at the mouth of a gallery running off to the right of the track, and the car had run upon a turntable at the entrance thereof."

Henry acted as tour guide for the magazine's writers and illustrators as they traveled through the underground chambers. At one point the men came upon "a car filled with ore and propelled by one of the miners, to avoid which they were compelled to scramble up on the foot wall and hold on by the timbers until it passed. The motive-power of the machine was a young man, black, grimed, and greasy, from a small oil lamp which he carried secured on his cap or turban, and which, from the position he assumed in pushing the car forward, threw faint light upon the track just before him…"

Based on newspaper and historical accounts of the time, these "black, grimed and greasy" workers, largely illiterate immigrants, spent a large amount of their non-work hours in drinking establishments like the tavern at the Mine Hill Hotel. What their lives were like outside of the mines, and what they talked about while knocking back cheap booze at these licensed and unlicensed establishments in Irishtown is, sadly, lost to history. These were not the type of men to keep journals, or write long, detailed letters which might survive today. But a glimpse into the lives of miners in Irishtown—or at least of how they were perceived by the local press of the day—survives in accounts of a notorious but now long-forgotten crime that briefly made Mine Hill the center of national attention.

CHAPTER THREE

The Cox Hotel and the murder of Mary Ann Moore

Five years after *Harper's* published its account of the workings of Northern New Jersey iron mines, Henry Conklin Byram sold the property at the intersection of "the road from Crane's Corner to the Dickerson Mine" and "the road to Dover" to Thomas Cornelius, the man for whom the current business is named. Cornelius paid $1,232 for the property in 1865 (the equivalent of $14,409 today), and held it for eight years. An 1868 map of Mine Hill is the first to show an actual structure at the location (there is no similar indication on an earlier, 1853 map), accompanied by the notation "T. Cornelius."

Byram lived another sixteen years after selling the property, dying on February 15, 1881. In the local *Jerseyman* newspaper of Friday, February 18, a page three item recounted the deaths of four Dover residents, imbued with a personal tone absent from modern obituaries: "Mr. Henry C. Byram was the last of the four, whose death occurred about noon on Wednesday. He died of cancer in his face, from which he endured untold suffering."

A year or so prior to Byram's death, the steam engine which had given the Byram Mine its brief fame was consumed in a fire. That ended the peak time for the Byram Mine, and operations were finally shut down in 1883. Byram's wife, Emily, who was co-owner of the property upon which the Mine Hill Hotel was built, outlived her husband by 33 years, dying in August of 1914.

Though the Cornelius name would be resurrected in the late 20th century, emblazoned on the signage of the property he had owned 120 years earlier, very little is known about Thomas himself. At the time of the purchase of the property, Cornelius was about 45 years old. A miner and farmer who was born in England, Cornelius and his wife, Elizabeth, owned real estate and other property valued at $2,100 in 1870, which would be about $30,000 today. Though hardly wealthy by the standards of the Dickersons or the Byrams, the Cornelius' weren't lacking in resources.

A document found at Morris County Surrogate Court indicates that Cornelius was a Mine Hill resident when he died on June 8, 1883, leaving his wife, Elizabeth as his only known heir. When county officials questioned Elizabeth as to whether there were other heirs, she told them, according to the Surrogate Court document, that "Cornelius did have by his former wife two children, and that at that time said Cornelius lived somewhere in the West, but that no definite knowledge of the names or Post Office address of said children can be ascertained..." Elizabeth reportedly said the children had not been heard from "for ten years past" and that she "cannot ascertain if they, or either of them, are now living."

In 1868, fifteen years before Cornelius died, James Cox took out a lease on the property where the former Mine Hill Hotel now stands, for $150 a year, the equivalent of $2,017.50 today (or about $168 a month in current dollars). A lease agreement dated March 4 of that year required Cox to "farm the land in a good and husband man like manner and not remove or sell or dispose of any hay, grass, straw or cornstalks raised or grown over said leased premises and...to keep all the fences in good repair..."

The lease agreement also says that Cox has the right to build "a frame building to be used as a store house or dwelling house" on a corner of Cornelius' property "in front of the Store House of Joseph C. Harvey." On the 1868 map of Mine Hill that first pinpoints the Mine Hill Hotel, there are two structures that are located across the road from the property. Situated on opposite sides West Randolph Ave., both structures are labeled Harvey—on the south side of West Randolph Avenue is a structure labeled "J.C. Harvey," and on the north side, where the Mine Hill Hotel parking lot is now located, is a structure marked "Mrs. Harvey." One of these structures is clearly the Harvey "Store House" described in the Cornelius/Cox lease agreement. In the 1860 census, Joseph Harvey lists his profession as "merchant."

Joseph Harvey's store is long gone now, as are almost all of the other businesses that came into being in Mine Hill's post-Civil War years. But the little country hotel and tavern that James Cox built on the intersection of the "road from Crane's Corner to the Dickerson Mine" and "the road to Dover" managed to hang on, in various incarnations, for the next 135 years. Not surprisingly, the property first went by a rather obvious name, The Cox Hotel (or, alternately, Cox's Hotel).

In May of 1869, James Cox was granted his first "License to keep an Inn or Tavern," at the Cox Hotel location. On his application for a tavern license, Cox had to obtain the signatures of at least twelve "reputable" local land owners "who have not to the knowledge or belief of deponent recommended any other application for a license to keep an Inn or Tavern, therein to sell vinous or spirituous liquors within a year."

Further, land owners (or Freeholders in the parlance of the day) by their signatures certified that Cox "is a person of good repute for honesty and temperance, and is known to us to have at least two feather beds more than are necessary for his family use, and is well provided with house-room, stabling and provender."

Among the individuals willing to recommend Cox for his tavern license were his landlord, Thomas Cornelius, the aforementioned Henry Conklin Byram and Augustus C. Canfield, the attorney nephew of Mahlon Dickerson who was the secretary and general manager of the Dickerson Succasunny Mining Company, secretary and treasurer of the Ferromonte Railroad Company, and an incorporator of the Morris County Savings Bank. A year after he signed his name to the Cox tavern license application, he began serving a two-year term on the New Jersey Assembly and a few years later became a New Jersey State senator from Morris County.

In 1872 Augustus Canfield would again vouch for Cox on his license renewal application, and this time he would be joined by his brother, Edmund, a prominent mining engineer who was instrumental in the establishment of the High Bridge branch of the Central Railroad.

The lease between Cornelius and Cox originally had a term of five years, but the working relationship must have been an agreeable one, since in 1870 the two men extended the lease to as long as ten years.

Cox appears to have been a very industrious young man. In 1870, when at age 30 he was both operating the Cox Hotel and farming Cornelius' land, he listed himself in the federal census as a butcher, a trade his brother Bernard would take up himself in coming years. At the time Cox lived at home with his 60-year-old father (also named Bernard), and three brothers, the aforementioned Bernard (18), John (25) and William (16).

Interestingly, within the Cox clan were enthusiasts of the infant game of "Base Ball." An 1870 newspaper account of a ball game between the Mine Hill Base Ball club and the Cable club of Dover lists J. Cox as the second baseman for the Mine Hill team. It's unclear whether this J. Cox was James himself or his younger brother, John, but given James' responsibilities at the time it was more likely that John—a laborer and the younger of the two—was probably the ball player described in the newspaper piece. In any case, "J. Cox" was a pretty good player: He scored four runs, including a homer, during the 1870 game described in the Morris County *Jerseyman*. John and James' brother Bernard Cox was on the team as well, as the pitcher. Bernard scored two runs for the team that day.

What's intriguing about all this is that the very first baseball game had only been played twenty-five years earlier, in Hoboken's Elysian Fields in 1845. These were the days when news traveled incredibly slowly (by today's standards). Base Ball, while gaining popularity, was far from "the national pass time" it is today.

Remarkably, for nine years after that first ball game was played in Hoboken, there were only two teams of record playing the game, according to "The Jersey Game," a history of baseball in the Garden State, by James DiClerico and Barry Pavelec (1991). The 1854 season was the first where four teams—the Knickerbockers, Eagles, Gotham and Empire clubs, all based in Manhattan—competed against each other. Just four years later about fifty teams competed in the New York metro area, with another sixty junior or "muffin" teams feeding players into the senior teams.

"The year 1860 saw a general blossoming of the New York game," DiClerico and Pavelec wrote. "The top teams were taking advantage of the growing railroad networks to spread the game and their fame throughout the East. Team tours brought attention to the sport and launched heated intertown rivalries, which had never existed before."

With regular train service from nearby Dover into Manhattan, it's not much of a stretch to think these rail tours might have been exactly how Mine Hill sports enthusiasts first discovered Base Ball. It's certainly true, based on later newspaper accounts, that "heated rivalries" took place between the Mine Hill Base Ball club and nearby towns like Boonton and Stanhope. Mine Hill was a tiny community of a few hundred people at the time, yet their Base Ball team made pretty good showings against teams from a much larger cities.

The *Jerseyman* weekly newspaper of Morris County reported on the Dover vs. Mine Hill game in which the Cox brothers played. Here is the *Jerseyman* item, edited slightly for clarity:

Although the score was large, the game was an exciting one. The score, at the end of the 3rd inning, was 12 to 10 in favor of the Cable [club]. At the end of the 5th inning the tables were turned, the Mine Hill [club] leading, 20 to 19. At the 7th inning the score was even, but [during] the next two, the Cables made 15 runs to their opponents 8, finally winning, 43 to 36.

Other players on the 1870 Mine Hill team have names that would be familiar to anyone with Irish ancestry: Lucas, Cormony, Colligan, Maloney, Grady. It's not hard to imagine the players strolling over to the Cox Hotel after the game, to be treated to a few beers by the pitcher and second baseman's older brother James.

The Cox Hotel had been in operation for about three years when, on the morning after Thanksgiving, Friday, November 29, 1872, news of a sensational crime swept Irishtown, and the hotel played a cameo role in a drama that captivated the Northeast.

Two teenage boys, the brothers McElhearn, were out tracking rabbits on the morning of the 29th when they came upon the bloody, semi-nude body of Mary Ann Moore a few feet from Jackson Brook. She was face down in the snow, with one arm extended over her head and her upper body positioned on a slight rise before the brook. Her feet were so close to the stream that they were almost touching the water. A trail of blood and footprints on the snow-covered ground led directly to the house Mary Ann shared with her miner husband, Solomon David (or "Dave") and young son Davey. The McElhearn boys immediately ran for help and Jackson Brook quickly became overrun with Irishtown residents who wanted to see the body.

It seemed, in fact, that nearly everyone in town had at one time or another gone down to Jackson Brook that day to take in the gruesome scene. Everyone, that is, except the deceased woman's husband, Dave Moore, who spent the morning at Terrence and Bridget Connelly's place. The Connellys ran an unlicensed boarding house and tavern out of their home, located on a two-acre farm about a half-mile from the Cox Hotel. Both Mary Ann and Dave had been regulars there for close to ten years. Moore had shown up that morning dressed in clothes different from those that he had worn the night before, when he had also spent time at the boarding house. On arriving there Friday morning, Moore told Bridget Connelly that "my wife is gone."

Thinking that he meant that Mary Ann had gone to the county poor house, Bridget made little of the remark. But when 16-year-old John McElhearn rushed into the Connelly house to report the existence of the dead body by the brook, Bridget's suspicions were immediately aroused. According to her later testimony, she turned to Moore and said something to the effect of, "Go home, Dave. You might have done something wrong."

But Moore didn't return home. Instead he began a days-long flight from the law. One of the last people to have seen him in Mine Hill that day was Bridget Maloney, a neighbor. According to *Jerseyman* newspaper accounts of the trial that followed, Maloney testified that she saw Moore coming out of the Connelly house that day, and the two carried on what appeared to have been a mild flirtation.

"He was well dressed and looked pretty good," she testified at Morris County Courthouse. "He said, 'Good morning, Mrs. Maloney.' 'Good morning,' says I. He said, 'You are singing pretty early.' I was singing at the time." Like many others in town that day, Maloney went down to the brook about an hour later, after her son told her about the body. She then went to the Moore house, which was a few dozen yards from the brook, and found the interior literally covered in blood.

Described in the press as "a fearfully dilapidated shanty, no more than a barn, and the midst of squalor and filth that were perfectly awful," the Moore house had clearly been the site of a terrible struggle. A pair of blood-soaked overalls was found in the house, which were obviously Dave Moore's. He became the prime suspect in the crime.

The Moores' young son was detained as a material witness and a police search for the older David Moore began. Doctors Thomas Crittenden and Isaiah Condict, both of Dover, performed a post mortem examination of Mary Ann's body on November 30th in the Moore home, which was standard procedure at the time.

Crittenden later described Mary Ann as being "of frail make, about 35 or 40 years old." There were several incised wounds on her face and head, including one stab wound that penetrated her brain and another that nearly sheared off her lower lip. "The woman was of delicate condition," Crittenden said, "and had been very much exposed to the weather."

A blunt instrument like a club made other wounds on her body, the doctor testified. These wounds were numerous, including on her arms, legs, chest and head. One of her ribs had been broken.

Within a few days, Moore was arrested in Phillipsburg by Dover Constable John Armitage and jailed in the county seat of Morristown pending trial. Because of the gruesome nature of the murder, the crime made headlines across the state and even appeared on the front page of the *New York Times* on February 13, 1873.

Moore gave a series of jailhouse interviews in which he declared his innocence and said that another man, Thomas Madden, also a miner, was largely responsible for Mary Ann's death. After one such interview, the Morris County *True Democratic Banner* reported that, "after a debauch of several days [Moore] determined to sober up and on Thanksgiving morning remained about the shanty with his wife, who had visited a neighborhood bar." When Mary Ann came home from the bar, she was quite intoxicated and "in company with Thomas Madden." Madden was also intoxicated, and Moore was "induced" by his wife and Madden to go to the saloon to purchase a quart of liquor.

According to Moore's account in the *Banner*, he went to Connelly's (alternately spelled "Conley's"), where he became intoxicated himself, and staggered home. He told the newspaper that, "Entering the house he found his wife struggling with Madden, who she affirmed had violated her and afterward had kicked and beaten her." Later, in his testimony at the Morris County Courthouse, Moore said that upon returning home he "caught Tom Madden right on top of her." According to Moore, Madden quickly got off of Mrs. Moore

23

and grabbed a butcher knife to ward off her husband. As Mary Ann was telling her husband what had happened, Madden reportedly gave her two more kicks and held the knife over her head in a threatening manner. Moore said he tried to force Madden to leave and begged him not to kill Mary Ann. He also "went over to her to pull down her clothes to cover her nakedness."

Oddly, according to Moore's testimony, things then suddenly calmed down, with all three taking a few drinks and, even more bizarrely, Madden suggesting that the three of them go to bed together. "I am no beast," Moore reportedly told Madden, "I won't go to bed with you and my woman." Then Madden's mother showed up, asked for a drink and was told it was all drunk up already. According to Moore's testimony, Madden's mother told Madden to give Moore a dollar for more booze and sent Moore out to buy another bottle.

Mind you, $1 was a lot of money in 1872. Throughout the late-1800s, miners wages in the area fluctuated between $1 and $1.60 per day, most often lingering in the lower regions of that pay scale.

After having spent Madden's dollar on himself instead, Moore—according to his own court testimony—returned home even more intoxicated about an hour before dawn. There he found his wife badly bruised and bleeding. He placed her on the bed and waited till daylight before asking her how she was. "Tom Madden beat me," Moore said she told him. He then claimed he carried her to the brook to wash the blood from her, but he was still intoxicated and fell and dropped her a couple of times, once on a large jagged rock, injuring her further. He claimed that she died there at the brook, in his arms. He then went home and changed his clothes. Afterward he returned to Connelly's, where he stayed for an indeterminate amount of time. When Mary Ann's body was discovered, he fled first to Dover, then to Rockaway, Newark, Jersey City, New York, briefly back to Mine Hill, then eventually to Phillipsburg, where alert police officers arrested him.

During all of the alcohol-induced violence on Thanksgiving night and the following morning, the Moore's adolescent son Davey never even came home. He was too busy was running all over town with his pals, stopping at Connelly's himself, sleeping in a stack of hay, visiting a Mine Hill store, and spending some time at the Cox Hotel tavern.

When the case came to trial, the Morristown courthouse overflowed with spectators. Before the first word was said in Moore's defense, the press of the day seemed to have made up its mind about who had killed Mary Ann Moore. Dave Moore was described by the *Jerseyman* as having "the appearance of a criminal of the lower class, ignorant and degraded. One looks in vain in his countenance for any evidence of intellect or refinement."

The *New York Times* said Moore "presented the appearance of a dull-minded, but rather vicious man."

Testimony was heard from many residents of Irishtown who knew the defendant and the deceased and could trace their whereabouts during the night in question. They described Moore as a likeable man when sober, but abusive when intoxicated. Seven witnesses testified that he had beaten and threatened his wife in the past.

These witnesses included Bridget Grady, who testified that about a month before Mary Ann's death, she had seen Moore kick her in the side and stomach and break a fiddle over her head. "We didn't dare go near her to assist her," she said. "I helped wash the body after her death, saw old black and blue marks on her, and she often deserved beating, too. I don't like to be too hard on him."

On cross-examination, Bridget was asked why she felt Mary Ann "deserved" the beatings: "She deserved it because she didn't attend to her work and was often drunk. She may often have brought punishment on herself."

Bridget Connelly testified that Moore had told her that if his wife died, he would "bury her under a rock."

Edward Travers testified that he had seen Moore hold Mary Ann by the hair while he kicked her: "He told me it was none of my business if he killed her, and I ran away to save myself from his violence. Moore said that he would have my life or his wife's life before night."

Moore's attorney tried to down play the spousal abuse charge: "That the prisoner had misused his wife was of no account; such things were common occurrences in Irishtown, where probably nearly every man beat his wife. We must imagine ourselves on a level with the people in order to understand the case."

The prosecutor had a field day with Moore's testimony: "Moore gives you the idea that there was hostility between Madden and Mrs. Moore, and that as Madden went down there to rape her, and had not succeeded, he had killed her. Did Moore do the natural thing when he found Madden in criminal intercourse with his wife, and hears his wife crying murder? He rushes in and what does he do? In a few minutes, to use his own words, 'we cooled off, and we all took a drink together.' Impossible, gentlemen! Impossible!"

When Madden testified, he claimed that he had gone to Moore's house after having spent the day drinking with him at Connelly's. At the Moore residence, they talked about mining affairs and then Madden passed out on the kitchen floor near the stove. After Madden's mother came by, he went home with her and stayed home the rest of the night. On Friday morning Madden continued his bender, drinking at several establishments, including the Cox Hotel. Then he went to an uncle's house and remained there for a week. In his account of Thanksgiving Day and the morning after, Mary Ann Moore does not even make an appearance. Not surprisingly, Madden's mother, Margaret Quaid, backed up her son's story, saying she didn't know where her son had spent Thanksgiving day, but found him passed out at Moore's house that night and took him home. She hadn't seen Mary Ann that night, either.

The prosecutor's conclusion was that Mary Ann had been murdered after Madden had already left the Moore home, and pointed out that the overwhelming circumstantial evidence pointed to Moore as the murderer.

In his summation, Prosecutor F.A. DeMott said, in part, "In a degraded place as Irishtown was, David Moore seemed to be more brutal than any of the rest. We have shown how his wife ran to the neighbors for protection against her husband. Have proved his threats to kill her, and proved Tom Madden's absence from Moore's house that night, and that Moore was left alone with his wife. All the evidence shows that Moore and his wife were the only two living creatures in that house that night. In the morning, Mary Ann Moore's dead body was found by the brook thirty or forty yards from the house."

Moore's attorney, J.J. Cutler, disputed DeMott's case and pinned the murder on Tom Madden: "Madden is left alone with Mrs.

Moore, and now that David has gone, he expects to satisfy his passions...Two fires burn in Madden's breast, one lit up by the liquor, the other by his passions, and the lustful deed is accomplished."

He dismissed testimony that worked against Moore's case. He attempted to show discrepancies in the prosecution's evidence. He even alleged a conspiracy within the community against Moore, based on his religion. Moore, he said, "heard threats of vengeance against him. These threats were against the Orangeman, the Protestant Irishman of the community, and made by the Catholics banded together against him."

None of this seemed to carry much weight with the jury. In February of 1873, it returned a verdict of second degree murder, and Judge Darymple sentenced Moore to twenty years. The *Jerseyman* newspaper opined, "The verdict of murder in the second degree was doubtless founded by the Jury upon the general idea that abusing and pounding their wives is a sort of entertainment to which the people in that locality are accustomed, and that the woman was either physically unable to stand the usual amount of beating or kicking, or Moore was so excited and drunk that he did not grade it properly. They believed he did not mean to kill her, but merely to punish her severely. But whoever reads the testimony must draw the conclusion that a state of society exists among the lower classes of foreigners who find employment in the Mines of our county that calls loudly for repression. It is terrible—heart-sickening and loathsome to the last degree. And unless justice is administered with a stern and unrelenting hand, such scenes of violence and blood will be every-day affairs by-and-by."

To say that the attorneys on both sides of the Moore murder case held the citizens of Irishtown with a certain level of disdain is stating the obvious, as it is to say the press of the time was unfairly biased against those same citizens. Accounts of the Moore murder trial in the papers of the time would have their readers believe that the immigrant population of Mine Hill were all ignorant, violent drunks, wife-beaters and sexual deviants. While it's certainly true that impoverished, disenfranchised immigrant populations often experience higher levels of alcohol abuse, depression, and domestic violence than the general population, those societal ills have been linked to the dearth of opportunities and sense of hopelessness with which these populations are faced rather than anything endemic to the people themselves.

The religious, sporting and cultural life of Irishtown citizens was largely ignored by the press that covered the Moore murder, but the Irish immigrants of Mine Hill were apparently active in all of those facets of life. The *Dover Iron-Era* regularly reported on church activities in town, for example, such as the "fair and English tea party" given by young congregates of the Mine Hill Presbyterian church in the spring of 1879; or the oyster supper held to benefit its minister, Rev. Pearce Rogers, which netted an impressive $102; or the "very interesting sermon" by a visiting priest from Stanhope that drew a standing-room-only crowd at the local Catholic church, St. Mary's in neighboring Port Oram (now Wharton), which was founded in 1845 specifically to serve the needs of the iron mining community. The aforementioned Presbyterian Church was founded in 1874 and for many years its minister, Rev. Rogers—himself a former Welsh miner—was known "to enter the depths of the mines to administer aid to the injured and consolation to the bereaved families that suffered loss of father or brother through some sad accident."

Despite the hysterical rantings of the *Jerseyman*, murder did not become an "every-day affair" in Mine Hill by any stretch of the imagination. Neither did it vanish altogether, however. Less than a decade and a half after the Moore sentencing, James Cox's brother Bernard would be on the witness stand himself, in an 1887 murder trial that would nearly eclipse the Moore trial in its level of sensationalism.

Six months after the Moore verdict came down, on August 1, 1873, the now-married James Cox bought the property upon which he'd developed the Cox Hotel—along with much of the surrounding land—from Thomas Cornelius. Almost immediately afterward, the Coxes had all of the former Cornelius land mapped out by Civil Engineer Andrew Rossi and had it divided into lots. Apparently other portions of Cornelius property now owned by James and his new wife Julia were also being leased by outside individuals. On the day of the Cornelius-Cox sale, William Matthews of Randolph Township and

Warren Painter of Rockaway began paying rent to the Coxes that they had previously paid to Cornelius.

Then, after owning the Cornelius properties for about a year, the Coxes began selling off various plots of the land. On April 8, 1874, they sold a parcel designated as "lot 3" on the Rossi map to Elias White, of Dover. Two other lots went to Randolph Township's Morris Delaney on the 20th of the same month. And on the 24th New Yorkers Anna and James Morrow bought still another lot. On June 24 Alonzo DeCamp of Bridgewater also bought some of the former Cornelius property.

On May 23, 1874, the Cox Hotel itself was sold to Randolph Township's John Bone, who gave the property the newly macabre-sounding monicker, "Bone's Hotel." On September 26, 1874 Bone applied for a tavern license, which was granted on October 12. Among those signing his application as character witnesses included Thomas Cornelius, Augustus C. Canfield and Canfield's brother, Frederick A. Canfield, another nephew of Mahlon Dickerson who went on to a prestigious career.

Along with a license application, innkeepers and tavern owners of the time were required to sign an "Innkeeper's Bond," which committed the tavern owner to maintain an orderly establishment and to respect the letter of the law. A painful financial penalty was inflicted against those Innkeepers who are unable to keep a respectable drinking establishment.

On his Innkeeper's Bond, Bone acknowledged himself indebted to New Jersey in the amount of $100, which would be levied against him if it was found he allowed disorderly conduct by his patrons or permitted gambling on the premises. The fine could also be levied against him if it was found that he failed to provide sufficient lodging for customers and stabling for horses.

In addition to the tavern proprietor, a co-signer was often required on an Innkeeper's Bond. The co-signers had to commit themselves to the tune of $50 to ensure that the licensee would respect state and local laws pertaining to the operation of inns and taverns. These were substantial amounts of money in late 19th-century America. One hundred 1874 dollars is the equivalent of almost $1,600 today, so the co-signer was most likely a close friend or business associate of the licensee.

During the early 1880s, Bone often co-signed an innkeeper's bond for James Matthews, the owner of the Port Oram Hotel in what is now Wharton but was then a part of Randolph Township. In return, Matthews co-signed for Bone. Sometimes each signed for the other on the same day, so it's clear the two men had some sort of mutually beneficial relationship.

After purchasing the hotel, Bone took up residence in an upper floor with his wife Nanney, six children and possibly two other family members. During their residence at the property, the Bone family nearly became the victims of one of the strangest and most frightening incidents to ever occur at the hotel.

Around midnight on a mid-June Sunday in 1881, Hugh Quinn—about 36 years old and employed a late-shift weekend iron miner from Ireland—was walking to work when he noticed a strange light in the rear of Bone's Hotel. Thinking it was just a kerosene lamp, he continued walking on until he realized that there were loud crackling sounds emanating from the property. Running back to the hotel, he began pounding on the door to alert the occupants, who awoke to find a small part of their home on fire. After quickly extinguishing the fire, it became clear to Quinn and the Bone family that they had nearly been the victims of arson. A small amount of paper, kindling and kerosene had been used to deliberately ignite the fire, and, in addition, kerosene had been splashed on the door to the stairwell that led to the Bones' apartments. If the fire had not been extinguished in time, flames would have blocked the only exit from their home, and the entire family would likely have perished.

Wrote the Mine Hill correspondent for the *Dover Iron-Era*: "No one who saw the fire place the next day can doubt that it was the work of an incendiary. For the sake of human honor, nobleness and probity I would gladly think it an accident were it not the evidence of a cowardly guilt so plain. And again is it possible that there is in this community a person who harbors in his heart a revenge so diabolical in its nature as to prompt him to sacrifice the lives of ten helpless human beings in order to satiate some imagined or perhaps real injury? Let us try to think otherwise."

The fire remains a mystery to this day. If a police investigation followed, there is no record of it. The Randolph Township Police Department maintains its records for seven years before destroying them, and the *Iron-Era* didn't follow up its report with any further details in later editions.

John Bone had owned the hotel for about seven years when the arson occurred. Just two years later, on August 12, 1883, Bone died while still owning the hotel. Morris County Surrogate Court papers show that he had only made out his will two months earlier, on June 12, leaving everything to his wife, Nanney. One could speculate—given the brief time between the filing of his will and his death—that Bone suspected the end might come rather soon. He may have decided it was important to get his estate in order because he found out he was terminally ill, for example. But it's impossible to know without a death certificate or an obituary in the local papers, neither of which were able to be obtained. It's also likely that Bone died there in his family's apartments at Bone's Hotel. While today a majority of Americans live out their last days in hospitals, that wasn't the case in the 1880s, when births and deaths occurred far more frequently in the home.

After his death, his body would have been cleaned and dressed in his best attire by the female members of his family and displayed on a table in his residence, all of which was customary at the time. Family and friends would have then dropped by to pay their final respects and raise a few glasses in toasts to the deceased. The fact that his wake was held above or within a tavern in a neighborhood that was made up predominantly of Irish immigrants might lead one to think there was a good deal of drinking going on at the time. The Irish, after all, have always viewed a wake as a time of gaiety mixed with sadness.

According to the website AllAboutIrish.com, "The Irish have always loved a good party and the wake, like any other gathering in the community, became an occasion to share food and drink, have music and dancing and to enjoy some physical games. At various times in the past there were efforts by Church officials to discourage the raucous events but they were generally unsuccessful."

Given all indications, John Bone probably got one heck of a sendoff.

After Bone's death, his hotel fell into the hands of his wife, Nanney. As the executrix of her husband's will, Nanney sold the

Bone's Hotel property to Elizabeth Ellis for $2,100 (the equivalent of $40,350 today) on November 5, 1883. Interestingly, Ellis was the mother-in-law of James Matthews, the Port Oram Hotel owner for whom John Bone had co-signed several innkeeper's bonds. Ellis did not run the Mine Hill Hotel property herself, but apparently leased it to two men over the course of the next seven years. James Berryman and John D. Kelly were licensed to operate the Mine Hill Hotel during separate periods from the early 1880s through the early 1890s and Mahlon E. Beam was the licensed proprietor just before the close of the 19th Century.

Interestingly, among the character witnesses for Berryman on the 1884 tavern license renewal form was Hugh Quinn, who had kept the hotel from burning down in 1881. Two other men who vouched for Berryman on his license application that year—Daniel O'Connell and Bernard Johnson—would have their own impact on the hotel in coming years.

It's entirely likely that the various individuals involved with the hotel at the time did quite well with the business. The mines were more active than ever in the 1880s, and a virtual parade of laborers must have passed by the front door of the saloon every day, at all hours, on their way to work. Newcomers and travelers were arriving in Mine Hill on a regular basis, and for many of them, their first stop would have been the Mine Hill Hotel.

CHAPTER FOUR

Corn hooks, ghosts and the drowning of Elizabeth Ellis

One would think that being the only legal bar owner in a town of several hundred working class individuals with a cultural tradition that embraces pub life would be a pathway to—if not wealth—at least a comfortable lifestyle. But it is evident that the owners of the Mine Hill Hotel were not operating in an environment that was completely free of competition.

Several unlicensed taverns thrived in Irishtown throughout the first few decades of the hotel's existence. The authorities often turned a blind eye to these properties, as many were allowed to continue for years without facing legal challenge. Others were less lucky, but enough continued operating through the peak iron period for Mine Hill (1860—1890) that it seemed that far more folks were drinking in "underground" booze joints than sipped the perfectly legal stuff at the Mine Hill Hotel. None of this could have made the proprietors of the hotel very happy.

Neither were the more sober-minded townsfolk or the rather morally high-minded local newspapers happy about the unlicensed operators in town. The *Dover Iron-Era* condemned the unlicensed taverns, calling them "a bane in our midst [that] breed drunken riots and fill our lockups with criminals." Just after Christmas, 1873, for example, the *Iron-Era* ran a small but telling item in the newspaper: "At Widow Connelly's unlicensed grog hole at Mine Hill, the last Sabbath day was disgraced by a drunken spree and brutal fight in which men (or brutes) stripped themselves naked to the waist. We learn that there are several parties in that neighborhood so addicted to drink that respectable people are determined to enforce strict measures against them."

One would think that the "Widow Connelly" was likely Bridget Connelly, who with her husband Terrance had operated the unlicensed liquor establishment that played such a big part in the Moore murder. But Terrance Connelly was still alive in 1873. Indeed, Connelly was one of fourteen individuals who signed as character witnesses on the petition to renew James Berryman's tavern license in

Matt Connor

1887. So either the newspapers erroneously described Bridget as a widow or there was another Connelly in town operating an unlicensed tavern at the same time.

One of the unlucky operators that actually got caught selling booze without a license was a rascally fellow named Patrick Fox. In February, 1876 Fox found himself dragged in front of a Dover judge by Marshall John Armitage (who also arrested Dave Moore back in late 1872). Fox, according to the *Dover Iron-Era*, "kept a little gin mill on Mine Hill," and after he invited a group of Irishtowners over to his "ranche" one Saturday, the group "indulged in a general drunk that lasted till about three o'clock on Sunday morning."

During this long, wild party, the quiet neighborhood townsfolk "were unable to sleep, for the night was being made hideous with the curses and yells" of Fox's customers, "whose anatomies had become perfectly soaked with Pat's crooked whiskey."

Fox had trouble keeping things under control, and a "whiskey riot" broke out, in which furniture was smashed, glass shattered, and counters and shelves ripped apart. Fox was half-drunk himself when Armitage hauled him in front of Judge Gage in Dover. Gage asked Fox if he had been selling booze at his house without a license. Fox answered that he was innocent of selling whiskey. He had been giving it away for free, you see, and was therefore not in violation of the law.

Since when did you become so wealthy that you can give away free cocktails to any and all that showed up on your doorstep? the judge asked. Fox's reaction, according to the *Iron-Era*, "was nonplussed" and the judge ordered him put in a temporary lockup for the night.

The next morning Fox was sufficiently contrite that the judge took pity on him and, hearing that he had not yet eaten, asked him if he had any money for a hot meal.

"Nary a cint, yer honor," Fox is said to have answered.

Gage "opened his naturally compassionate heart and bought him a nice warm meal," the *Iron-Era* reported, and then sentenced Fox to county jail in default of bail.

Before being taken into custody, a sheriff did a body search and found $38 on Fox's person, a considerable sum at the time (equivalent to about $640 today). Clearly these were the proceeds from the his recent liquor sales. So much for free booze and no money for breakfast!

Another unlucky tavern owner was the widow McDonald, who in the summer of 1878 also found herself in front of Judge Gage. In the early part of the week ending July 27, one Patrick O'Brien went before Gage with a complaint against "the widow of Michael McDonald" (her first name was not mentioned), whom O'Brien claimed was operating a "disorderly house" at the time. O'Brien said he was walking by the place when Mrs. McDonald "who does not like him for some reason" encouraged her raucous customers to chase O'Brien down.

O'Brien managed to get to his home safely, but the gang surrounded his house, banged on his doors and shouted obscenities at him. Warrants were issued on eight of Mrs. McDonald's customers identified by O'Brien.

Called before the judge herself, McDonald admitted that she sold alcohol without a license and, the *Dover Iron-Era* contended, "it is alleged that she has kept about her a number of immoral women, which together have made her house a wretched place." She was immediately sent to county jail.

"Notwithstanding that she has recently lost her husband and that she is soon to become a mother, she seemed perfectly indifferent about the matter," the *Iron-Era* reported. "[she] said that the jail was a place she was curious to know, and that the county would soon have to keep two instead of one."

In the fall of 1886, an allegation much more serious than illegal alcohol sales or the hint of prostitution was leveled against the operator of another local liquor establishment. Daniel O'Connell was proprietor of what the Morris County *Jerseyman* called "a low saloon at Mine Hill," when his life was torn apart in what the local newspapers referred to as "The Corn Hook Tragedy."

In 1880 O'Connell, then a 34-year-old Irish immigrant and farmer, had applied for a license to operate a tavern out of his home on what is now West Randolph Ave. near Thomastown Road, a quarter mile from the Mine Hill Hotel. Though is application was rejected, O'Connell continued to run his illegal tavern for several years. Oddly, in 1883 O'Connell was the first to sign as a character witness on Mine Hill Hotel proprietor James Berryman's innkeeper's license application (which, by the way, was granted in May of that year). A year later, in 1884, O'Connell again certified to Berryman's fitness to operate a tavern in Mine Hill. The fact that O'Connell was signing off on Berryman's license is ironic considering that during the same period O'Connell was apparently flaunting the law by operating his own illegal gin joint just down the street from Berryman's establishment.

According to the Morris County *Jerseyman* newspaper, on September 30, 1886 O'Connell was arrested for killing a miner named John Smith. Smith, 24 and of Scottish heritage, was walking across O'Connell's property en route to the Dickerson Mine, where he was an underground engineer, when the incident occurred. Part of O'Connell's three-acre farm had at one time had a horse-and-wagon path through it, which led to the mine. Locals were known to use that path to traverse back and forth on a regular basis, until O'Connell grew tired of having his vegetables tramped upon. He put up a fence to close the route off, only to find that folks would simply remove the crossbars from the fence in order to continue using the old wagon path. Sometimes, O'Connell alleged, they forgot to replace the crossbars, and cattle would cross onto his property and consume his crops. At some point or another he had a conversation with Smith about this very matter. He said he gave Smith permission to cross his property as long as he didn't use that particular route across his potato field.

O'Connell continued to have trouble with cross-traffic and disabled fences, and was told by a neighbor, "John Thatcher," that Smith was the cause. "Thatcher" is a fascinating character in this story. In the later trial he was painted by O'Connell as a troublemaker with some kind of grudge against Smith. In fact, "Thatcher" is alleged to have encouraged O'Connell to sue Smith for, presumably, destruction of property. Because of an embarrassing allegation made against "Thatcher" (mentioned below), his name has been changed here in deference to his surviving descendants, many of whom still reside in the Mine Hill area. Intrepid researchers can easily ferret out his real name in old newspaper accounts of the time, if they so desire.

Thatcher, O'Connell later recalled, "would come to me day after day and tell me what the Smith family had done about the fence."

On the other hand Thatcher claimed that O'Connell had threatened Smith in the past. He said O'Connell had told him (in language censored by the local papers) that he "would kill that Scotch—of a—if he went that way [across his fields] again."

Damaging to Thatcher's account was his admission that O'Connell had once had Thatcher arrested for an act of indecent exposure in O'Connell's home.

In any case, it's clear that Smith was indeed crossing O'Connell's property at the time of the incident, and that the route was taking him across O'Connell's potato fields. At the time of the incident Smith was wearing a heavy leather miner's cap and was carrying his dinner pail with him. A confrontation occurred and Smith ended up dead, stabbed in the head with a corn hook, a tool for cutting corn from cornstalks.

In his testimony before the jury in Morristown the following January, O'Connell said he had asked Smith to take a different route to work, and that Smith had behaved in an openly hostile manner, immediately throwing a punch and almost sending O'Connell to the ground.

"You [expletive]," Smith is alleged to have said to O'Connell during their altercation. "I was long looking for you." Smith was described as a having been a big man who stood six feet tall and weighed a muscular 180 pounds. O'Connell claimed to have been intimidated by the larger man: "He looked bigger and madder than I had ever seen him before," O'Connell testified. "He struck me on the jaw on the point near my ear. The blow partly knocked me down."

O'Connell then testified that Smith lunged at him a second time, and this time O'Connell held up the corn hook to defend himself. Smith impaled himself on the knife and then fell to the ground, O'Connell said, where he died less than an hour later.

With few phones in the area in those days, O'Connell said he then ran to the Dickerson Mine and asked the foreman, James Binney, to call a doctor.

Binney gave key testimony during the trial, in which he described O'Connell's mood just minutes after the incident occurred.

"O'Connell asked me to phone a doctor," Binney said on the witness stand. "I asked what was the matter and he said, 'phone' first and he would tell me afterward. I did so. Then he said Jack Smith was in the habit of crossing his potato patch. The potatoes were all out, but that didn't matter. He told him to go back, but he wouldn't; he pushed him and then Jack struck him; he then raised the corn hook and Jack ran into it. O'Connell said at first he was mad. He said he put no heft to the blow...Smith did not die till fifteen minutes to half an hour after I got there."

But the notion that O'Connell simply held the corn hook, "putting no heft" to it, was somewhat disputed by Dr. Isiah Condict, who performed the autopsy on Smith (and was also one of the doctors who had performed the post mortem on the late Mary Ann Moore 14 years earlier). He said the wound that killed Smith penetrated through the leather miner's cap the young man was wearing, pierced his skull and went two inches into his brain. So the corn hook seems to have been wielded with some force.

Locals alerted to the scene did their best to treat Smith's wound until a doctor arrived. Smith was bleeding profusely and vomiting. Twice local folk moved his body so he would not be lying in his own blood and vomit. One local man wrapped a stone in a piece of cloth and placed the stone on the wound on the side of Smith's head, to try to staunch the bleeding. Later Smith was bandaged and covered in a blanket to keep warm.

None of this did much good, of course, and by the time Dr. John L. Taylor arrived on the scene, Smith had been dead for at least fifteen minutes. He was buried in a Succa Sunna cemetery after a funeral at the Presbyterian Church in Mine Hill, officiated by Rev. Pearce Rogers.

"It would take a blow of considerable force to penetrate the hat and make such a wound," Taylor said later.

In order to establish a timeline of the events leading up to Smith's death, O'Connell's attorney quizzed O'Connell and several witnesses as to what O'Connell had been doing just prior to the corn hook incident. It turns out that one of the last people to see O'Connell prior to the death of John Smith was Bernard Cox, the brother of Cox Hotel founder James Cox, who was now a butcher. He had sold some eels to O'Connell at about 4 p.m. that afternoon, less than an hour prior to the corn hook incident.

"The first thing I done after dinner I talked to Bernard Cox awhile and bought some eels from him," O'Connell testified.

Cox testified that around 4 p.m. (it may have been a little earlier or a little later), he had sold "a mess of eels" to O'Connell, adding that O'Connell said he was in a hurry, that he wanted to cut corn.

O'Connell claimed he was on his way out to his fields to do just that at the time he encountered Smith, who allegedly behaved so volitilely toward him. Slung over one shoulder was a bag of apples O'Connell was going to deliver to a neighbor, Helen Branch. In his other hand was the corn hook.

Disputing O'Connell's account of the incident was Mary O'Toole, who rented a cottage from O'Connell on Thomastown Road and said she witnessed most of the incident from her back porch. During her testimony, O'Toole claimed that she had seen no aggression by Smith. Indeed, she said, Smith had apparently tried to put the breaks on the situation by calling out, "Hold on, Dan." She claimed that O'Connell dropped his bag of apples, grabbed Smith by the shoulder and struck him with the corn hook unprovoked. Her testimony was quite damning.

The next day Branch's husband found the bag of apples and brought them to his wife. But the bag was stained with Smith's blood, and, Branch said, "I could not use the apples for the thought of the thing."

Testifying in favor of O'Connell was his hired hand, whose story generally corroborated O'Connell's, though he admitted that his view of the altercation was partly obscured by a barn and a significant growth of corn, and that he was unable to hear what the two men had said to each other.

Observing the court proceedings was "the aged father of John Smith," who occupied a seat beside Prosecutor Willard W. Cutler. In its account of Smith's funeral, the *Dover Iron-Era* described Smith's parents as "aged and stricken."

On the witness stand, O'Connell admitted that he had previously been convicted of operating a "disorderly house," a profession he practiced for five or six years, until just four months prior to the incident with Smith.

The jury was retired on Thursday, January 13, 1887 at about 12:15 pm. Later interviews with jury members determined that initially five had stood for murder in the first degree, five for murder in the second degree and two for manslaughter. By 6:35 p.m. the jury reached agreement and returned a verdict of second degree murder. O'Connell, the newspapers reported, was "greatly disappointed" with the verdict, as he had "confidently believed that the jury would acquit him and allow him to return to his home a free man."

At his sentencing, O'Connell pled for mercy from the court, pointing out that his wife and eight children would be left with no means of support if he was sent to jail. The judge sentenced O'Connell to 15 years hard labor regardless.

Sadly, the story doesn't end there. John Smith's grief-stricken father, who had witnessed much of the testimony at his son's trial, was only to survive his son by three years. The elder Smith, like his son, was also a miner, and in 1889, a horrific mining accident sent John Smith Sr. to his own grave.

From the *Boonton Weekly Bulletin*, November 14, 1889, under the headline "Buried in the Mine": "John Smith, father of the young man who was killed by Dan O'Connell several years ago, was buried in the Dickerson Mine, in the old workings, on Tuesday morning of last week. He and his son-in-law went into this mine to work taking out the top ore; there was a plank roadway over an abandoned ore bed, and as Smith was wheeling a barrow over the plank the ground above it caved in. The hole was in the shape of a funnel, and as poor Smith went down more earth and rock came after, thus completely covering him out of sight. His body may be down several hundred feet, and it may not be so far. But as this part of the mine is an old working, it is impossible to say where his body is located. The men were at work Wednesday with ropes and ladders, and also timbering, to see if they could get his body, which is under tons of debris."

A team of miners, including foreman James Binney—who had provided key testimony at the Daniel O'Connell murder trial—tried desperately to retrieve Smith's body. But the task became increasingly dangerous, and, The *Dover Iron-Era* reported, "All resources having been exhausted, the search for Mr. Smith's body has been abandoned and it will never be recovered."

The Dickerson Mine closed for good a little over a year later, in 1891. According to Marjorie Kaschewski's 1973 book, "Hosts of Ghosts in Northern New Jersey," the Dickerson Mine area off Canfield Ave. may be haunted by the ghost of an old miner buried alive with his wheelbarrow just before the mine's closing.

In 1987 journalist Ric Medrow revived the story in a sidebar to a larger piece on the history of Mine Hill which appeared in the local *Randolph Reporter* newspaper: "It is said that those strolling off Canfield Avenue after midnight might hear the creak of the wood and iron wheelbarrow, or worse, see the bent figure pushing his prized wheelbarrow from the Dickerson Mansion site to Drury's Corner," Medrow wrote. The "Ghost of the Dickerson Mine" tale was dusted off again in 1998, when the local historical society included an account in their booklet commemorating the 75th anniversary of the town's cessation from Randolph Township.

Could this miner's apparition, now thought to be roaming Canfield Avenue for over 100 years, be the unquiet spirit of John Smith, still grieving over the murder of his young son, pushing his wheelbarrow across that unstable wooden walkway for all eternity?

If so, he might not be the only specter who haunts Drury's Corner, located about a quarter mile west of the former Mine Hill Hotel. Those who love a good ghost story might be interested to know that Mine Hill residents of the late 1870s and early 1880s were apparently terrorized by the apparition of "a woman in white." According to newspaper accounts of the time, she was seen regularly on that corner during the time period. Interestingly, the tavern at the Mine Hill Hotel would therefore have been easy walking distance from the two overlapping ghost sites. Some might say that the existence of a popular drinking establishment so close to two allegedly supernatural locales might go a long way to providing a rational explanation for the bizarre visions.

On April 26, 1879, the *Dover Iron Era* ran the following report from its Mine Hill correspondent: "I do not approve of inserting a ghost story, as an item of news, in my correspondence, but as there has of late been an excitement that is a little beyond the common order, among the credulous portion of our people, resulting from a silly ghost-story, I will not this time deem it improper to include it in my communication."

According to a story related to the *Iron-Era* correspondent by one of his sources, a local woman at the time was getting regular visits from a ghostly "woman in white." Over twenty years previous, in the late 1850s, this same local woman had emigrated from England. While in that country, she and a female childhood friend with whom she "had been on the most intimate and confidential terms," made a vow to each other: The first one to pass away should "appear spiritually" to the other.

Today such a vow might seem a bit strange or morbid, but the 1850s saw the peak of the spiritualist movement, when interest in ghosts, seances and contacting the dead was at its height. Statements like those made between the two friends in England were not terribly unusual among spiritualist believers of the day. Even the famous escape artists and spiritualist debunker Harry Houdini promised his wife that if he could contact her from the great beyond, he would do so, using a specific code.

In any case, years passed after the vow was exchanged between the two English friends, and the local Mine Hill woman completely lost contact with her childhood companion. Then one night in early April of 1879, she was awakened in the dead of night by the touch of a cold hand upon her forehead.

"Terror stricken, she opened her eyes, and there before her bedside, looking pale and deathly, stood the friend and companion of her childhood," the newspaper reported. Deciding that she must be dreaming the whole thing, the woman tried to rouse herself from sleep but found that she was already quite awake.

"The spectre silently stood by her bedside, staring at her with deathly eyes, and at length took her hand and said in a mournful tone, 'I come to fulfill the pledge that I have ever held sacred. I will meet you at the midnight hour tomorrow night.'"

On the following night the apparition appeared at the appointed time, and apparently showed up repeatedly thereafter.

A later report from the *Iron-Era*'s Mine Hill correspondent suggests that a "well-known 'gentleman' of this place" might have been perpetuating a hoax by dressing up as the woman in white. Later still the newspaper attributed the ghostly visitations to the "hallucinations of some inebriate." Nonetheless, for a few years after the tale of the "woman in white" first started making the rounds, the intersection of Canfield and West Randolph Avenues became known as "Ghost's Corner." Indeed, that was the common nickname for the area prior to the erection of Peter Drury's house on that spot in 1882, which gave the location its current monicker.

Was the "woman in white" merely a hoax? Was she simply an alcohol-induced hallucination? And what of the miner ghost? During journalist Medrow's brief investigation into its existence, he spoke to Bob Behrent, described as "a local expert in unexplained occurrences." Behrent was quoted as saying, "Since I have never been told of this legend, it may be just that, a legend."

Legend, fact or inebriate's fantasy? No one can say for sure.

As the 1880s gave way to the 1890s, Mine Hill went through a turbulent time marked by multiple mine accidents, unlicensed tavern activity, the occasional ghost sighting or unexplained fire, and the rare but not unheard-of homicide. But there was one more incident to come that would shock and sadden Mine Hill residents before the year 1890 reached even its halfway point.

Over in the neighboring Port Oram section of Randolph Township—since renamed Wharton—lived James and Elizabeth Matthews, who operated a local hotel and tavern there. James Matthews, you may recall, was at least somewhat acquainted with former Bone's Hotel owner John Bone, who had co-signed innkeeper's bonds for Matthews in 1880, '81 and '82. Upon the Bone's death in 1883, Elizabeth Matthews' mother, Elizabeth Ellis, purchased the hotel from the Bone estate. Ellis was already past seventy at the time she bought the hotel, and had some experience in hotel and tavern operations since she often tended bar at the tavern of her son-and-law's Port Oram property.

From the time of her purchase of Bone's Hotel until her death, Ellis apparently leased the hotel to James Berryman and John D. Kelly, both of whom were granted tavern licenses in town at the time. Kelly even placed a prominent advertisement in the 1888-89 Morris County Directory: "Kelly, John D, Mine Hill Hotel, newly refitted, new proprietor, fine wines, liquors and cigars."

Still, considering her knowledge of bar operations it's unlikely Ellis stayed away from her Mine Hill property for very long stretches, and it's even conceivable that she may have occasionally stopped in to tend bar at the Mine Hill Hotel's tavern. Today it's possible to drive from just about any location in Mine Hill to just about any location in Wharton in about five minutes or less. In the 1880s Ellis would have had to walk or take a carriage when travelling between Port Oram and Mine Hill, but the trip would still have been a reasonably easy one.

A beloved local character, Ellis took great pride in her belief that, in her late seventies or early eighties, she was the world's oldest living bartender. She was warm-hearted and quick to lend a hand to her neighbors and most in the area referred to her simply as "Grandmother Ellis."

On a mid-May morning of 1890, residents of Port Oram and Mine Hill were saddened to hear she had died as a result of drowning. Early that morning, a young boy was wandering along the eastern edge of the Morris Canal when he came across an article of clothing floating in the water. Calling out to the captain of a dredging boat nearby, he pointed out the clothing: "Say, somebody's throwed a dress in the canal, and they're foolish, too, for it's a good one." Turning his attention to the spot indicated by the young boy, the captain realized it was actually the body of an elderly woman that was floating in the water.

Later newspaper accounts of Ellis' death vary somewhat, as do their accuracy. One newspaper referred to Ellis' son-in-law as "Charles Matthews" rather than James Matthews. Another described Ellis as "the wife of the hotel keeper at Port Oram," rather than as his mother-in-law. Depending on the newspaper, Ellis died either on Sunday, May 18 or Monday, May 19 and she was either 79 or 81 years of age (the birth date on her gravestone is 1811).

The *Dover Iron-Era* had the longest and most detailed account of Ellis' demise, under the headline, "An Aged Lady Drowned: Mrs. Ellis, of Port Oram, wanders into the canal during the night." In this account, it was said that the 79-year-old Ellis' mental faculties had been on the decline, and that her daughter and son-in-law had taken her to England recently to seek treatment. When they returned to America, however, they found that Ellis' health was not greatly improved. The newspaper claimed that Ellis' language was "childish at times, indicating that her mind was becoming enfeebled."

This account has Ellis' body being discovered on a Sunday morning, Ellis having been last seen by family members around midnight Saturday. James Matthews was reported to have checked all doors to make sure they were securely locked before going to bed that night, but in the morning a hotel boarder found the rear door of the building wide open.

"From all the circumstances it was very evident that Mrs. Ellis in a period of derangement of mind had gone out of the house quietly and had wandered into the canal," the *Iron-Era* reported.

The *Jerseyman* had a somewhat different take on Ellis' death, however. That paper claimed that Ellis, at 81, was "lively and clear-headed," but that her son-in-law had hired some new personnel at the hotel and had told Ellis that her bartending services were no longer required.

"Recently Matthews thought he needed a man to wait on his customers, and the old lady was told she might pass her days in peace and rest. She brooded so over the deposition that she became ill," the newspaper reported.

Monday morning, the *Jerseyman* reported, Ellis failed to report for breakfast, a search was initiated and her nightcap was found floating in the canal.

The *Jerseyman*'s conclusion was that Ellis "had gone out in her night dress and committed suicide."

After a brief inquiry, the local coroner decided an inquest was unnecessary and released Ellis' body to the family for burial preparations. Ellis' funeral service was held at her former residence, officiated by Rev. Joshua Mead of Chatham, Rev. Charles Larus of Port Oram and Rev. Pearce Rogers of Mine Hill. She was buried in Rockaway Presbyterian Cemetery.

In her will, Elizabeth Ellis bequeathed all of her property to James and Elizabeth Matthews, "particularly the hotel property known as the John Bone Hotel on Mine Hill...which I recently purchased of Nannie Bone, executrix of said John Bone."

The Matthewses held onto the property for about eight years before selling it to Dover residents Annie and Richard Barrett for

$1,500 (the equivalent of $32,280 today). Richard was a 42-year-old New York-born manager of a beef house. Annie was a housewife fifteen years his junior. Barrett appears to have been a man of some resources, as he supported not only his wife but also his mother-in-law, sister-in-law and a niece. The Barrett home also housed a boarder and a servant.

Like Elizabeth Ellis, the Barretts appear to have leased their property rather than run day-to-day operations themselves. During the late 1880s and 1890s John D. Kelly was licensed to operate the Mine Hill Hotel, but on April 29th, 1899 Mahlon E. Beam applied for a license to operate the property. The license was granted on May 2, and on Friday, May 26, Beam held a grand "reopening ball" at the hotel. Remarkably, a poster advertising this event survives today.

"There will be good music in attendance and accommodation for horses and wagons. Come one, come all and have a good time," the poster reads.

Prior to the grand reopening ball, either Beam or the Barretts hired the Brooklyn artist D.M. Spencer to paint a large mural on the wainscoat wall behind the bar in the hotel's tavern and dining area. The folk art painting depicted the U.S.S. Maine battleship with Old Glory waving at the front of the ship and tiny sailors scattered about on deck.

The sinking of the U.S.S. Maine in Havana Harbor in February of 1898 caused a furor throughout the nation in the waning years of the nineteenth century. The Maine had been the pride of the US Navy, the first fighting ship designed and built entirely by American Naval architects. It was in Havana Harbor that year to provide a place of refuge for Americans in Cuba during a period of high tension on the island.

For centuries Spain had controlled Cuba, which had frequently been racked by unrest as Cuban natives fought for independence from the European power. Americans received regular reports, via the sensationalist press, of Cuban rebels' intense suffering at the hands of the Spanish government, and of the frequent rioting was taking place there.

"By 1898, the feeling between the United States and Spain had settled into a quiet, mutual antagonism, with Yankee sentiment almost entirely on the side of the Cuban insurrectionists," wrote John Walsh in his 1969 book, "The Sinking of the USS Maine."

At around 9:30 p.m. on the evening of February 15, 1898, an explosion ripped through the Maine, killing 267 crewmen. The sensationalistic U.S. press immediately leapt to the conclusion that a Spanish mine had caused the Maine disaster, and called for war. The rallying cry of "Remember the Maine!" was used to incite patriotic Americans across the nation. Wild talk of retribution filled the air. American investigators, however, were unable to conclusively determine the cause of the explosion, leading a few more sober-minded members of society to question the wisdom of going to war over an incident that seemed to have no clear explanation. Spanish authorities, of course, denied they had anything to do with the U.S.S. Maine explosion.

The denials by Spain and the calls for clear-headed caution by a few Americans only led to more strident arguments, more wild claims by yellow journalists. War, it seemed, was inevitable, and indeed followed, in April of 1898. It's not hard to imagine the fervent dialogues about the war, the Maine, and the Spanish-American political situation that might have taken place over shots of whiskey and glasses of beer at the tavern at the Mine Hill Hotel.

Like the triggers for all other American wars, from the Boston Tea Party to the attacks on the World Trade Centers on September 11, 2001, the sinking of the U.S.S. Maine in 1898 was an event that seared their hearts and minds of Americans everywhere, so that years later many would still remember the incident with anger and passion.

That was certainly true in the little village of Mine Hill, where a local tavern keeper chose to immortalize the event on the wall of his establishment. How long the painting remained in view is an open question, but it had been forgotten for decades when it suddenly re-emerged in beautiful, vivid color one day deep in the twentieth century, a stunning and delightful surprise to the a whole new generation of Mine Hill residents.

CHAPTER FIVE

Trouble for Treible, abounding bootleggers and the shooting of Pat Gallagher

As the 19th Century gave way to the 20th, a new sense of hope and excitement was dawning in America. Technologies like Mr. Edison's electric light were brightening even the more rural areas of the country. The telephone, phonograph and automobile would soon become commonplace in the homes of the upper and middle classes. Massive steamships navigated the oceans at faster and faster speeds.

It was during this bright, enlightened time that, in tiny Mine Hill, NJ, Annie and Richard Barrett sold the Mine Hill Hotel to a Pennsylvania couple, Austin and Louisa Treible. Unfortunately the experience the Treibles had at the hotel could hardly be called bright and successful.

The Treibles had moved to New Jersey from East Stroudsburg, in Monroe County, PA, where they were a fairly prominent family. Today the Monroe County telephone directory contains two full pages of listings for Treibles in the area.

Owners of the property for nearly ten years—from 1902 through 1911—the Treibles initially took out a loan in the amount of $2,250 to pay for the property (the equivalent of $46,557.69 today), with a mortgage to be held by the Barretts until paid off. This loan was secured from Carrie S. Reid, a prosperous resident of the Boston suburb of Newton, Massachusetts. Reid had moved to Newton with her physician husband after their marriage in 1878, but she had been born in Morris County and prior to her marriage had lived in nearby Rockaway.

Why Reid provided the loan is an open question, but $2,250 was a price significantly higher than that paid by the last few owners. At the same time several market forces were at work which may have prevented the Treibles from making the little hotel economically viable. The couple didn't help matters any by driving themselves deeper in debt. In 1908 they took out a second mortgage on the Mine

Hill Hotel, in the amount of $585 (the equivalent of $11,656 today), from Christian Feigenspan, a corporation of New Jersey.

Christian W. Feigenspan was a multimillionaire Newark banker and brewer whose Feigenspan Brewery was one of the largest and best-known in the state until prohibition forced him to shut down operations, costing him, by his own account, $3 million (the equivalent to almost $27 million today). The fact that he weathered such a staggering financial blow and continued to thrive in other business endeavors demonstrates his remarkable versatility. When prohibition was lifted during the first Presidential term of Franklin Roosevelt, Feigenspan reopened his brewery and prospered until his death in 1939. Today Feigenspan beer labels, bottles and other memorabilia are highly sought-after by collectors.

Feigenspan's resources were vast. Besides the brewery, he was president of the Federal Trust Company and had investments in real estate, coal and ice. The *Newark Evening News* reported that he once personally underwrote a deal to the tune of $1.3 million, which caused him about as much concern, the newspaper wrote, as an offer to light a friend's cigarette. Given his importance in the business world, it's unlikely he personally had anything to do with the Treibles, who would have been small potatoes to him. It was one of his companies that provided the $585 mortgage, but when the Treibles later got into trouble with their creditors, that $585 was enough to draw the Feigenspan company into a bit of trouble as well.

Despite the difficulties to come, however, the Treibles began their ill-fated Mine Hill Hotel adventure with a flourish. They hired John T. Price, a noted photographer based on Blackwell Street in Dover, to capture the property on film, the earliest photos known to have been taken of the hotel.

One such photo shows the entire front of the property, looking essentially the same as the current structure, demonstrating how little additional exterior construction has been done on the hotel since the turn of the century. Standing in front of the property, in the entrance to the tavern, are two gentlemen and a dog. One man wears a bowler hat and carries a rifle. The second is in shirtsleeves and a vest much like bartenders wore at the time. Only this gentleman's right arm appears to be intact: His left arm stops a few inches below his shoulder. Local historians have taken to calling this man "the one-armed bartender" and speculate that he may have lost his arm in a mining accident.

The second photo shows a group of men and children gathered in the exterior railed walkway on the second floor of the property. An imposing- and prosperous-looking man stands at the center of the picture, dressed in a tie and vest, with a watch chain dangling from a vest pocket. Because of his air of authority and his placement in the photo, some believe this man is the proprietor of the hotel, Austin Treible himself. To the right of this gentleman stands a younger man in a suit and bowler hat, grinning broadly and pointing to the man believed to be Treible. Lined up on either side of the two central figures are eleven other gentlemen and four small children, the smallest of which is held by the man believed to be Treible. With the passage of nearly a century and no identifications visible on the photo itself, none of the figures in the photographs can be conclusively identified, however.

Unfortunately for Austin, Louisa and the other businesspeople in town who were dependent on the local iron mines to stay afloat, Mine Hill's place in the iron industry was on the wane by the turn of the twentieth century. Of the 22 mines that may have been worked in Mine Hill through the 1800s, only three continued in operation into 1900. Two of those three would be closed by 1902. The third would continue on through the 1960s, supplying later tavern owners with enough hard-bitten customers to keep the place in the black for the duration.

The reason for the decline of the industry in town had to do with the cheaper and more easily accessible iron sources discovered in the Midwest. But whatever the reason, Mine Hill was soon largely left behind by both the iron industry and the miners who worked in it. The population of Mine Hill plummeted as laborers went in search of work elsewhere, and the miner's cottages that filled Irishtown suddenly went vacant. This was, of course, a terrible situation for the tavern at the Mine Hill Hotel, which was known from the first as a "miner's bar."

Another large customer base for the hotel was stagecoach travelers. But the news on that front wasn't terribly good, either. After the turn of the century, the few surviving stagecoach lines began to vanish completely. With rail service throughout the county, stagecoaches rapidly slipped into irrelevancy. Adding insult to injury, the Morris County Traction Company (MCT) began trolley service from downtown Dover in July of 1904.

The trolley service carried travelers from Dover through Mine Hill and Kenvil and on to Lake Hopatcong with many stops in between. In other words, the MCT took over the role that stagecoaches had played previously by shuttling travelers back and forth between areas without rail service and those accessible by train. If the trolley had followed the probable stagecoach route that had run past the Mine Hill Hotel, the Treibles might have had a fighting chance. It didn't. Instead it followed the path of the current Route 46 through town, completely bypassing the hotel.

"The climb up Mine Hill along present-day Route 46 presented the stiffest challenge to the MCT," Larry Lowenthal and William Greenberg wrote in their 1984 book on the trolley service. "The trolley's ability to ascend steep grades allowed it to reach many communities that were inaccessible to railroads."

Charming as they were, and as beloved in memory as they are today, the trolley's brief tenure in the history of transportation in Morris County drove one final nail in the coffin of another much beloved transportation resource, the stagecoach. And more and more—without the crashing wheels of the coaches, the thunder of horses footfalls, the blare of the driver's horn—the little property on that once-busy intersection of Randolph and West Randolph Avenues began to take on an out-of-the-way, hole-in-the-wall quality.

Then, one year after the Treibles purchased the hotel, Henry Ford incorporated the Ford Motor Company, proclaiming, "I will build a car for the great multitude." In October 1908, he did just that, offering the Model T for $950. Eventually nearly 15.5 million of the automobiles were sold in this country alone. The development of an affordable automobile sounded the death knell for horse-drawn transportation in the U.S. and, for that matter, the trolley as well.

With buses and automobiles crowding out trolley service, the Morris County Traction Company went into receivership two decades after it launched the first trolley from Dover to Hopatcong, and stopped operations for good in 1927. The previous trolley routes along portions of present day Route 46 became dominant roadways in the area, permanently siphoning traffic off of Randolph Ave and West Randolph Avenues.

But there was still more bad news to come. About the same time the Treibles bought the Mine Hill Hotel, competition came to town. In 1882 a 35-year-old miner named Bernard Johnson bought a piece of property about a half-mile from the Mine Hill Hotel on what is now Randolph Ave. About twenty years later, when mine work was drying out and Johnson's children would have been grown, Johnson built an inn on the site, naming it the "Hotel Clara."

Like the former Mine Hill Hotel, the former Hotel Clara still stands today. Unlike the Mine Hill Hotel, however, Hotel Clara—today known as Joann's Bar—appears to have been so radically altered over the ensuing century that, except for the foundation and basement, it probably bears little resemblance to the original structure.

In an intriguing footnote to this story, the Hotel Clara might never have been built were it not for a single chilling twist of fate. In the early months of 1880, a hideous accident occurred at the Dickerson Mine, crushing a 30-year-old miner to death under a huge quantity of dirt and ore. As dutifully reported by the *Dover Iron-Era* newspaper, the miner suffered a ghastly death.

"Thos. Madden, a miner in the Dickerson Mine, was instantly killed at about eight o'clock on Wednesday morning," the paper reported in its February 28, 1880 edition. "He was at work loosening some ore when a quantity of rock and dirt gave way, and before he could escape from it, completely crushed him and terribly mangled his person. Among other injuries his brains were dashed out and scattered about."

If the name of this miner sounds familiar, it's because he's the same man who was accused of the rape of Mary Ann Moore on Thanksgiving day, 1872, and was known to have had a drink or two at the then-named Cox Hotel the morning her body was discovered. Madden, however, had not even been scheduled to work in the mines that day.

According to the paper, "A singular circumstance of the affair is that [Madden] was that day working as a substitute for…another miner."

The name of that other miner? Bernard Johnson. Because he stayed home from work that terrible day in 1880, Johnson cheated death and went on to develop the Hotel Clara in 1902, a business that remains in operation 100 years later.

Another mining accident—occurring about ten years after Madden's death, and at another mine in town—resulted in another miner's ghastly head injury. This miner, John Reilly, survived his injury but was reportedly never the same again. Depending on whom one believes, this terrible brain injury may have led, twenty years later, to yet another homicide in Mine Hill. This murder, which occurred during the eighth year of the Treibles' ownership of the local tavern and hotel, was once again fueled by alcohol and marked by spousal abuse. But this time the spousal abuser was the murder victim.

Pat Gallagher, a Dover man, was alleged to have been a nasty and abusive drinker. On Saturday, October 15, 1910, he reportedly forced his wife and their young child, Bessie, from their home after throwing a lamp at them. Mrs. Gallagher (whose name never appeared in the press) and her daughter caught the last trolley car to Mine Hill, where her brothers James and John Reilly lived in what the Morris *Daily Record* called "a small frame cottage surrounded by woods" in the Scrub Oaks section of town.

The *Record* interviewed little Bessie for a story that appeared in its October 17 edition.

"Papa had been drinking before he came home Saturday night and was angry," Bessie told the newspaper. "He told mama that she could not sleep there. Mother and I were getting ready to go to the home of Uncle John and Jimmie when pap picked up the lighted lamp and threw it at us, partly hitting mama. We took the last car from Dover and went to Mine Hill."

The paper also quoted a Mrs. Catherine Flynn, who was Mrs. Gallagher's sister. She described her brother-in-law as "ugly and a brute of a man."

Mrs. Gallagher and Bessie spent the night at the Reillys' while Pat Gallagher continued his bender. According to newspaper accounts of the later trial, Gallagher met up with Mine Hill resident William

Churn at 7 a.m. Sunday morning, and Churn drove Gallagher home in his horse-drawn wagon.

"I took him to his home in Dover," Churn testified, according to the *Daily Record* coverage. "We were there about five minutes. Then we went to Reilly's house about 9 o'clock. We went in and saw Jim, but I don't remember seeing John. Jim came with us and we went to Landing, Lake Hopatcong."

Upstairs in his room, John heard Gallagher and Churn arrive at his home. He had seen Gallagher in Dover the night before, he later testified, and they had been civil to each other.

"My sister came to the house about 10:30 that night," John Reilly would testify. "Sunday morning I heard Gallagher. He was asking where his wife was. She was in my room and I sent her down. He was talking about money to her."

After about twenty minutes, John Reilly said, Pat left with Churn and his brother.

"It seems that Pat didn't want to go but they coaxed him into it," John Reilly said.

When Gallagher, Churn and James Reilly arrived in Landing, Churn remained with his wagon while Gallagher and James Reilly went to the tavern of a local hotel for a few drinks. After about an hour, the three men set off again. On the way home from Landing they stopped at the Day's Hotel in Kenvil and Churn put up his horse in the hotel's stable. Churn then "went down the railroad tracks," presumably to his own home. James and Patrick then continued on foot back to the Reilly home in Scrub Oaks.

Under cross-examination, Churn said he had never spoken to Gallagher prior to that day, but had known the Reillys for quite some time.

"I have always known Reilly and wouldn't have gone to his place had Gallagher not asked me," Churn said. "He told me his wife was up there but he did not say why. I think she got kind of mad at him."

Interestingly, both James Reilly and Churn had a connection to the Mine Hill Hotel and its operators. As mentioned earlier, applicants for inn and tavern licenses at the time were required to obtain signatures from at least twelve individuals who owned property in the municipality in which the tavern or inn was located. These twelve individuals, by signing the license application, swore that the applicant is "a person of good repute for honesty and temperance" and that "such an Inn or Tavern is necessary and will conduce to the public good." The signers, therefore, would have to have had a familiarity with the applicant and the inn or tavern they operated. Both Churn and James Reilly had both signed tavern license applications for Mine Hill Hotel operators, Churn in 1907 and Reilly in 1900 and 1917.

"When I got home [from Kenvil], I took off my coat and sat down to dinner," James Reilly said when called to the stand himself. "I asked Gallagher to come in and eat but he said he wouldn't. He was sitting just outside the door, which was open.

"Gallagher was very angry with his wife and was growling. I got up and went to comb my hair, when Gallagher came running in and pushed me over against the rear of the house. He kept pounding me in the back of my head. Mrs. Gallagher came and helped me up. I was drunk, I admit, and couldn't get up.

"I then saw Gallagher leaning up against the outside of the door. He said he was going to kick the stomach out of his wife. I told him to quit it, but he said he'd clean house for the whole bunch. The next thing I knew he was shot."

John Reilly, who had been lying down in an upstairs bedroom, had been roused from bed when he heard his brother and Pat brawling.

"The next I heard was the racket in the house," John Reilly later testified. "Mrs. Gallagher said, 'Don't hurt him.' Then I heard Jim getting up. About five minutes later he told Jim if he had him outside he would kick him like a football. Jim said, 'I'd like to see you try it.' Gallagher said, I'll give you twice as much."

The dispute then apparently moved back outside. According to Bessie Gallagher's interview with the *Record* the day after the shooting, her father "chased mama into the yard and around a tree. While going around the tree he fell. Mama ran into the woods and back into the house."

Gallagher followed his wife to the entrance of the cottage and stood outside the doorway, according Catherine Flynn's interview with the newspaper. From his vantage point at his bedroom window,

John could clearly see Gallagher. He pulled a revolver from under his pillow, opened the window and shot Gallagher in the arm.

Gallagher started to run, then collapsed and began begging for some water. Perhaps surprisingly, James Reilly went to assist him: "It's not going to kill you, Pat, you are a husky man and can stand it," John Reilly told the stricken man. "I told [Pat] I would go for Charlie Wilcox and get a bicycle and go for a doctor. He asked for a glass of water first."

James Reilly was cradling Gallagher's head in one hand and holding a glass of water to his lips with the other when John Reilly walked over to Gallagher and fired again, putting a bullet in his head.

"Murder in Mine Hill," cried the Morris *Daily Record*, and once again Mine Hill residents flocked to the courthouse in Morristown to watch the proceedings. Reilly pled not guilty, claiming that he did not recall firing the second time and was not sure how the gun had discharged. It was pointed out during the trial that all three men had been drinking excessively during the night in question, and the Reillys claimed Gallagher had behaved violently toward both men on several separate occasions.

"After I shot him [the first time] I went downstairs and followed Jim, who was going toward Gallagher," John Reilly testified. "I didn't mean to shoot the last one. I did not shoot it. It went off. I intended the first but not the second. I had my hand over the gun and carried it at my side.

"I followed Jim back to the house and put the pistol back underneath the pillow. then I came down again and was going to Wharton to give myself up to Constable McDonald but Jim would not let me."

Prosecutor Charles A. Rathbun cross-examined John Reilly: "When you went down to Gallagher after the first shot, you went to finish him, didn't you?" he asked.

"No, sir, I did not mean to shot him again," replied Reilly.

Meanwhile, little Bessie Gallagher was unfortunately spared few details of her father's violent end.

"I heard the two shots and later saw my papa lying on the ground dead," Bessie told the *Record*. "I did not know it was him until Uncle Jimmie told me."

When Police Chief Ethelbert Byram arrived at the scene, he found Gallagher lying on the ground with a sheet over him and John Reilly calmly sitting in a chair.

"A very unfortunate occurrence has taken place here," Byram said to Reilly, according to his court testimony as reported in the *Record*. "In answer to me the defendant said, 'There's Pat. I had to do it in self-defense. If I did not do it, he would. I couldn't stand him chasing my sister.' John and James were both intoxicated. I took the prisoner to the Dover headquarters and then brought him to Morristown."

In his defense, Reilly's lawyer, former judge and state prosecuting attorney Willard W. Cutler (who had, coincidentally, prosecuted the Dan O'Connell murder trial nearly a quarter century earlier), alleged incompetence, pointing out that twenty years earlier John Reilly's head had been crushed in an accident at the Baker Mine, adversely affecting his mind.

Several witnesses testified that ever since the mine accident, Reilly had "acted queerly." The prosecutor had been prepared, with two physicians, to dispute the mental incompetence charge, but decided in the end that the evidence that Reilly was mentally unsound was too weak to hold water anyway. And indeed, on January 24, 1911 Reilly was convicted of murder in the second degree and received 12 years of hard labor.

Reilly was reportedly "greatly pleased" with the sentence, which was considered lenient. After hearing the jury foreman return the verdict, Cutler smiled at his client. Reilly smiled back.

Just two days after the Morris County newspapers published the verdict in the Gallagher murder case, another, less prominent item appeared in the local papers: "SHERIFF'S SALE In Chancery of New Jersey."

Whether because of difficult market conditions or other reasons lost to history, the Treibles were unable to make the Mine Hill Hotel a successful enterprise. After nine years as proprietors, the couple had barely made a dent in their first mortgage. Now instead of $2,250 (borrowed at a rate of 6% interest) the Treibles owed $2,376.87 (the equivalent of $45,670 today) to Carrie Reid, who was the lender in the Treible's purchase of the Mine Hill Tavern. Reid was listed as "complainant" in the Sherrif's sale advertisement placed in the local papers. The Treibles and Christian Feigenspan, a corporation of the state of New Jersey, were listed as defendants.

The Sheriff's auction was held in February 27, 1911, and Reid herself placed the highest bid, $2,000. According to the Morris County Sheriff's department, such transactions are fairly typical, though the amount of money bid by complainant (or plaintiff) Reid was unusually high. Usually—according to representatives of the Sheriff's department familiar with Sheriff's sales—a lender will foreclose on a mortgage and, if no significant bids are placed on the property foreclosed upon, will then bid a token amount at a Sheriff's sale—say, $100—and reclaim the property for later resale.

But if Reid was hoping to re-sell the property for a profit, why would she pour another $2,000 into it at auction, thereby increasing her stake in the hotel from $2,250 to $4,250—an exorbitant amount at the time (equal to $81,660 today)—which she could never hope to recoup?

Nearly 100 years later, there's no way of knowing why Reid tossed all of that good money after the bad. All that is known is that, on April 5, 1911, Sheriff Calhoun Orr signed over deed of the Mine Hill Hotel property to Reid and her husband, Robert, and the couple ended up owning the hotel for the briefest period of any owner, just three weeks.

Reid's odd course of business with the Mine Hill Hotel is doubly perplexing because of her background. Born Carrie Stickle, she was the youngest daughter of Barnabus King Stickle, perhaps the smartest and most influential businessman in Morris County of the mid- to late-1800s. A lifelong Morris resident, B.K. Stickle came from an old and distinguished family (Stickles were among the first settlers of the town of Boonton, for example), members of whom still reside in the Rockaway area, and who still maintain a proud family legacy.

In 1842, B.K. opened his first business, a small store next to a Morris Canal bridge in Rockaway. Over the next 33 years his business enterprises expanded to include shares in two local banks, investments in several large insurance companies and at least six railroads. He was a prudent and honorable businessman, well known in the county for his strong sense of integrity. Though not a churchgoer, he supported two local places of religion.

Like his father, Hubbard (who lived to the ripe old age of 97), B.K. had a robust constitution, and remained active until the last two years of his life, when a bad fall on the ice may have caused some kind of serious and lasting injury undiagnosable at the time. According to the local newspapers, after that fall B.K. complained of consistent pain in his right side. In 1875 he succumbed to some sort of internal malady, either "a diseased liver" or "an abscess [that] had formed which eluded the skills of his physicians, and the breaking of which caused his death."

At the time of his demise, Barnabus King Stickle was worth an estimated $500,000, an enormous sum at the time, equal to about $8.1 million today. As executors of his will, B.K.'s sons Byron and George Stickle claimed the bulk of the estate, with the rest of the family receiving annuities of various amounts. Carrie, one of three daughters, received $1,000 annually from the estate (the equivalent of $16,270 today) for the rest of her life.

Three years after her father's death, 24-year-old Carrie married Robert A. Reid, a physician from Marion, Indiana, and the young couple moved first to London and then Vienna, where Robert completed his medical studies. They moved to Newton, Mass. in the late 1870s or early 80s and raised three sons (one, Dr. William Duncan Reid, followed his father into medicine) and a daughter. Carrie's brother George, meanwhile, continued maintaining the family fortune, holding directorships at two local banks and an insurance company in which the family had substantial investments.

The Stickle family banking connection might partially explain why the Reids provided the $2,250 loan to Austin and Louisa Treible in the first place, though why she and Robert decided to invest more—obviously unrecoupable—funds in the Mine Hill property nine years later is still befuddling.

What is known is that on April 26, 1911, she and her husband dumped the property for $1,960, representing a total loss to them of $2,519.40, (or the equivalent of $48,322 today) including interest and legal fees. Here's hoping the tax structure in 1911 allowed for a substantial write-off!

Carrie lived an apparently prosperous life in Newton for the next eighteen years. During the early years of her marriage, she was socially active and took great interest in the establishment of Boston Symphony Orchestra. She died of a cerebral hemorrhage at her home on July 15, 1929 at the age of 74. Still a hometown girl, Carrie's remains were taken back home to Rockaway, for a private funeral and interment. Her husband, Robert—briefly the co-owner, with Carrie, of the Mine Hill Hotel—outlived her by just six years, passing away in February, 1935 at age 86. He was remembered by friends as "a good citizen—intelligent, public spirited, patriotic and honest."

Carrie's brother George had died three years previous, in 1932. He was the victim of an automobile accident caused by severe icing conditions resulting from what was described by the local press as "the most severe [storm] of the entire winter." The vast Stickle fortune, which had grown substantially since Barnabus King Stickle's death, was now valued at well over $1 million (or $13 million today), though it seemed to have undergone some shrinkage since the stock market crash of 1929. Because of this shrinkage, George's bequests were cut by 25 percent as a codicil to the his will. In the end, George remembered Carrie's children to the tune of $50,000 to $80,000 per person. Even reduced by 25 percent, her children benefited by between $492,000 and $787,000 in today's dollar value.

After the brief Reid tenure, David and Augusta Glass would become owners of the Mine Hill Hotel. Unlike the Reids, members of the Glass family would maintain ownership for over fifty years, longer than any other owner to date. The Treibles, however, would remain a regular presence at the establishment. The Glasses appear to have leased the Hotel to the former Pennsylvania couple, as Austin Treible's name would remain on tavern licenses associated with the Mine Hill Hotel for the next four years or so.

For the Glasses, this meant that the tavern would be operated by personnel already experienced in running the place. For the Treibles it meant their lives and careers could continue without significant change, presumably while paying monthly rent to the Glasses. On at least one occasion, David Glass recommended Austin Treible for a tavern license by signing off on his application and vouching for his reputation.

Matt Connor

While the Glass family brought a certain amount of stability to the property, their ownership would not be unmarked by tragedy or controversy. The large Glass family resided at 15 South Sussex Street in Dover for much of their ownership of the Mine Hill Hotel, a turbulent and unpredictable time to be a tavern owner in America.

With mining on the decline and—in their sixth year of ownership of the hotel—a World War sending much of the drinking-age male population off to Europe, it couldn't have been easy to keep the property out of the red. And things were not about to get any easier.

As late as 1915, Austin Treible's name continued to appear on tavern licenses granted to the Mine Hill Hotel. But early in 1917, the judges of the Court of Common Pleas—which was the body that then approved inn and tavern licenses locally—denied Treible a license due to a charge of sales of liquor on Sunday, which was then a violation of county ordinances. In the fall of that year his license was again denied.

"A similar application was denied February 2, 1917," begins a statement from the court dated October 9. "At that time, the reasons moving the Court were generally to the effect that the applicant's fitness did not appear in view of an accusation of Sunday selling, to which the applicant had pleaded non vult [or no contest]...and also the consideration of the community conditions that exist around and about the place proposed to be licensed."

Opposing the 1917 Treible license application were George Jenkins and a Reverend Hunter. Jenkins was the owner of the Jenkins, Buck & Co. General Store in Mine Hill, and a very religious community leader who had made substantial contributions to the local Presbyterian church. It's not surprising, therefore, that he would have been strongly against the sale of alcoholic beverages on Sunday, the traditional Christian Sabbath.

Though the judges gave Treible the benefit of the doubt with regard to liquor sales violations, they—rather oddly—failed to see a specific need in the community for an inn or tavern license for the property.

"Nothing appears upon this application to show that a second hotel is required or even desirable in the neighborhood," the court statement reads. "Nothing is offered to indicate that another licensed place would be justified under any reasonable view of the situation taken after the broadest application of principles that ought to receive attention from the viewpoint of community life and the public service."

In other words, the court said, Mine Hill was satisfactorily served by the operation of a single licensed hotel (the Hotel Clara, now Joann's Bar) and a second was simply not necessary. This flew in the face of history, of course. The Mine Hill Hotel had already been in operation for over fifty years when its license was rejected in 1917. Previous to 1917 the court had seen its way to routinely license both hotels.

The fact that two influential community leaders spoke out against the Mine Hill Hotel's application probably had a lot more to do with the denial of Treible's license than the existence of a second hotel in town. For how long the Mine Hill Hotel remained unlicensed is unknown. When a liquor license is revoked today, the owners of the revoked license are permitted to continue selling liquor while the ruling against them is under appeal. It's unclear what New Jersey law allowed in the early days of the twentieth century, but even if the property had continued to operate as usual in coming months, circumstances would soon arise that would again force its closure.

In March of 1918, some of the earliest cases of a particularly virulent, fast-moving and contagious strain of the flu were reported at the Fort Riley army base in Kansas. It was the beginning of a terrifying pandemic that would sweep the nation, leaving nearly 200,000 dead in its wake. Four months after the Kansas outbreak, public health officials in Philadelphia issued a bulletin about the so-called Spanish influenza. In September, Dr. Victor Vaughn, acting Surgeon General of the Army, received urgent orders to proceed to Camp Devens near Boston, according to a PBS "American Experience" documentary on the ensuing pandemic.

"I saw hundreds of young stalwart men in uniform coming into the wards of the hospital," Vaughn said. "Every bed was full, yet others crowded in. The faces wore a bluish cast; a cough brought up the bloodstained sputum. In the morning, the dead bodies are stacked about the morgue like cordwood." On the day that Vaughn arrived at

Camp Devens, 63 men died from influenza. Unfortunately, Vaughn was neither the first nor the last to be witness to such devastation.

In October of 1918, Spanish Influenza swept through New Jersey, resulting in tens of thousands of deaths. In his comprehensive paper on the influenza outbreak, "Mortality in Morris: The Influenza Pandemic of 1918," Richard T. Irwin wrote that Morris County suffered a higher death rate than any other county in the state. Before the pandemic had run its course locally—at the end of December of that year—6,512 Morris County residents would become sickened by the flu and pneumonia, and 641 would die from the diseases. On a percentage basis, 7.7% of the population of the county would be wiped out within an twelve-week period. During that brief window of time, more Americans lost their lives to the pandemic than on the battlefields of World War I.

In an attempt to stem the course of the pandemic, state officials forced the closure of all public gathering places, including saloons, dance halls, and ice cream parlors. For those twelve dreadful weeks, the tavern at the Mine Hill Hotel would remain dark, and its clear, vacant windows would be silent witnesses to an almost unimaginable horror.

For years before the influenza pandemic of 1918, and for decades afterward, Ida McConnell would call Mine Hill her home. Indeed, she lived about a quarter mile from the Mine Hill Hotel, in a former miner's cottage on Randolph Ave. Seventy years after the pandemic had run its course, this extraordinary 99-year-old woman would still be maintaining that little miner's cottage—the last intact miner's dwelling in town—in almost exactly the same condition in which it had been when she first set foot inside the home in 1912.

Pat Jones, a friend and neighbor of McConnell's for many years, often spoke with the old woman about her remarkable life.

"I would visit Ida almost every day, this was in 1984, '85, because I'd be taking my daughter for a walk and Ida would be out there in her front lawn, gardening," Jones said. "I became friendly with Ida because she was just so comfortable to talk to. Then I would just ask her to share some of the history of the town. She'd talk about the influenza epidemic of 1918, and she would constantly refer to this barn, a massive barn on the corner of East Randolph and Randolph

Ave., across the street from the hotel. She'd say 'That's where they stored the bodies from the flu epidemic.' It happened during the cold weather so they had to store the bodies somewhere. I don't know if it was a morgue or what."

Jones said McConnell told her of a horse-drawn cart that would roll down Randolph Ave., past the Mine Hill Hotel, and on past McConnell's own house, burdened with the corpses of flu victims.

"She said, 'Everybody was dying and this cart was coming down the street. I knew by the way the horses were slowly clip-clopping that I shouldn't go outside, because that's when the bodies would be there.' She said she would not go outside because she was afraid to see the pile of the bodies. The horse cart would first go to the barn opposite the hotel and then they would come down Randolph Ave. Then she said the cart would proceed all the way back down what is now Route 46 and pick up more bodies and make this whole trip several times a week. She said the pile of bodies would be so high, and the drivers would put a tarp over them, and the horses had some sort of a covering—a piece of cloth—over their face, and so would the driver. Sometimes, she said, before the cart would come for the bodies, people would die on Randolph Ave., right on the street. If there was a body on the street, Ida said, the townspeople would have to call the cart—I don't know how, because they didn't have a telephone—and they would come and pick up the body.

According to Irwin's account of the pandemic, 144 residents of Randolph Township, Port Oram and Dover would perish from the flu and pneumonia between October 2 and December 16, with the worst day of pandemic falling on October 17, when 40 Morris County residents would succumb to the diseases.

When the worst of the pandemic was past, state authorities lifted the ban on public gathering, and the tavern at the Mine Hill Hotel would have been allowed to open for business once more. While death became a less constant presence in Ida's life after that point, she would not remain untroubled by life's difficulties. Her husband Jess, while beloved by local children, was also a heavy drinker, for example. Ida consequently often found herself running down the street to the tavern at the Mine Hill Hotel to drag him back home.

"I had a nice married life," McConnell said as part of a videotaped interview in 1990, conducted for the Randolph Township Landmark's Committee Oral History Program. "Of course, everybody has ups and downs. I was no exception. But I had a pretty nice life. And I had a nicer life since [Jess] was gone. Because he drank, and I had worries. You don't know, a man gets one too many and you don't know if he's coming wrong or right. And he worked in Hercules [blasting powder factory in Kenvil, Roxbury Township], and that was a dangerous place."

Researchers who later restored Ida's home and its grounds as part of a museum told of finding scores of empty bottles in the ground beneath Ida's outdoor privy, indicating that Jess was probably running out to the outhouse for a snootful whenever he wasn't at the bar of the Mine Hill Hotel.

During part of her early life in Mine Hill, Ida recounted in the videotaped interview, the bar was known as "The Flamin' Rag" and a colorful local character made a name for himself with his unconventional entrances to the place.

"We used to have one man that had a horse, and he went off to the gold mines. I don't know where they were, somewhere," Ida told the interviewers. "And that hotel up there, he used to drive his horse right inside! He walked right up to the bar with his horse!"

McConnell lived into her 104th year, and in 1989 finally moved out of the perfectly preserved little miner's cottage she had called home for over seven decades. She had been a resident of Mine Hill since 1897 and was one of the last living embodiments—with her 97-year-old sister Elizabeth—of the town's rich history as an iron capital. In November of 1990, McConnell told the *Star-Ledger* that she remembered well the days when miners would head over to the tavern at the Mine Hill Hotel, which in 1990 was called Maddie's Mine Hill Tavern.

"The mines made the town a bustling place," she told the newspaper.

But the iron-mining period had largely come to a close in Mine Hill by the time the Spanish Influenza outbreak had run its course. Unfortunately for David and Augusta Glass—the owners of the Mine Hill Hotel at the time—the end of the health crisis in

December of 1918 was just a temporary respite. A little over a year later, in 1920, the Volstead Act became the law throughout the United States, and the tavern was legally prohibited from selling booze. It's unlikely, however, that a little thing like the 18th Amendment to the Constitution stopped the proprietors of the Mine Hill Hotel from providing liquor for their customers. Throughout Morris County, alcohol consumption continued at a pace that seems to have rivaled that of pre-prohibition days.

A perusal through microfilmed copies of the Morris County *Daily Record* for random periods of the 1920s (there is no complete index of the *Record*, and a review of all 4,500-plus issues of the paper from 1920 through 1933 was simply not practical) shows multiple accounts of Volstead Act violations. Indeed during certain periods, there were headlines every two or three days regarding alcohol-related incidents.

On October 5, 1926, for example, the newspaper reported on a liquor raid in Kenvil, resulting in the arrest of one Peter Taebeilli for the sale and possession of liquor. A little over two weeks later, Landing resident Frank McPeak was charged with illegal sale and possession, his second offense. On November 18 of that same year, Daniel Fichter was found guilty of selling booze at his poolroom and barbershop in Wharton. Previously, in September of 1926, a truckload of beer was seized in Wharton and the driver arrested.

Volstead Act violations relating to Mine Hill and its residents were also commonly reported upon in the local paper. The June 11,1924 edition of the *Record* contained an article on several raids made in the Madison and Mine Hill areas: "Mine Hill was the scene of the efforts of the Sheriff's men," the paper reported, "and they seized fourteen containers of liquor in the places of George Salso, Steve Capethak and George Kererko."

One month later, on July 11th of 1924, the newspaper reported that Warren County Constable Raymond Dalrymple was driving through Mine Hill when he was pulled over by a local cop, Stewart Bottoms. Turns out Dalrymple had recently led a raid on a hooch house in his own municipality but had failed to turn the booze over to local authorities. Instead he drove off with the liquor himself. It was still in his car when Bottoms pulled him over. Bottoms escorted Dalrymple and his party to the county jail, where bail was set at $500.

In September of 1924, Mine Hill resident George Vander Meulen was arrested on the Pine Brook-Parsippany highway while driving a truck that contained 22 cases of beer destined for a club in Dover. Indeed, accounts of Volstead Act violations in Dover are too numerous to list. Most of these violations occurred in hotels and taverns that had served alcohol during pre-prohibition days.

"Wholesale liquor raids were made throughout Morris County by the Prosecutor's detectives, assisted by the local police in different municipalities, on Saturday," reads a front-page story from the December 21, 1925 *Daily Record*. "Nine places were raided and a varied quantity of booze seized."

Today, an indication that the sale of booze at the Mine Hill Hotel and the former Hotel Clara continued through prohibition can be found below-ground, where, at both properties, hidden rooms still exist where local tradition has it that illegal alcohol was kept from the prying eyes of the authorities.

Such rooms were not uncommon in booze joints of the prohibition era. When police descended on a restaurant on the second floor of a Morristown building in 1925, for example, they were frustrated by not finding any booze at all, despite ample evidence that liquor had in fact been sold at the establishment.

"The search for liquor was unavailing, but Chief Wildey was not satisfied with the result that the men made a second visit sometime later," the newspaper reported. "It was then, hidden away in a store room on the first floor that the supposed liquor was seized. The police had quite a search for the cache but finally one peeking through a crack in the wall made the discovery of a sort of secret room where the liquor was."

Longtime residents said the tavern at the Mine Hill Hotel was rumored to have indeed been a "speakeasy" during the 1920s and early 1930s, though most surviving residents who were alive during the period were small children at the time, and would have only heard such rumors from their parents or older friends or relatives.

Lydia DeMarino, a lifetime Kenvil resident now in her late seventies, said that as a young child she heard many rumors about activities at the Mine Hill Hotel during the late 1920s and early 30s: "These were just stories you heard. I was just a kid at the time, but you remember things like that," she said. "I don't know if it was a house of ill repute or what it was. There were rumors about that. There were some high-steppers in that place. I never saw people coming and going. As kids we didn't get around very much, but there had to be some truth to the stories."

Added Albert "Abbie" Ebner, a lifelong resident of Mine Hill, "I think at one time it was a speakeasy of some sort. Hotel rooms available for people having trysts. A lot of transients. That sort of thing."

Given the amount of illegal activity that was going on throughout the county at the time, it would be surprising if the Mine Hill Hotel *didn't* sell booze during the period, for no other reason, perhaps, than just to keep up with the competition. John Curry, the proprietor of the former Hotel Clara, which in the 1920s and 30s was called "Curry's Pub," certainly seemed guilty of hootch sales.

On January 10, 1930, the *Record* reported that "Fines totaling $2,100 were imposed on Special Sessions Court this morning, all but $200 being for violation of the Prohibition Laws...Three fines of $500 each were imposed on those so sentenced being Rocco Citrese of this city, John Curry of Mine Hill and Frank Leary of Chester."

Curry was fined the maximum amount for a first-time offender, the paper reported. Does that mean he had not sold liquor previously? Not likely. He may have just been better at keeping the authorities at bay, or on his payroll.

In his book, "Jerseyana: The Underside of New Jersey History," Marc Mappen wrote about the challenges faced by Prohibition Bureau official Ira L. Reeves, who was responsible for enforcing the Volstead Act in New Jersey. Reeves aggressively fought bootleggers and speakeasy proprietors and had some success on that front for a while.

"Despite his successes," Mappen wrote, "Reeves was soon disillusioned. He was flabbergasted by the fact that everyone around him drank with abandon, from high school students to state legislators...Worse than the drinking was the pervasive corruption. He found that bootleggers were everywhere protected by the law enforcement authorities...His own office was a center of corruption. Agents who made no more than $3,000 per year were offered bribes of thousands of dollars a week."

Corruption was also found among prohibition officials in Morris County. On December 17, 1925, the *Record* reported that two former prohibition operatives who had been employed by the county sheriff's office entered no contest pleas to charges of extortion and conspiracy.

Raymond Tillotson of Boonton and Andrew McConough of Rockaway were charged with accepting a $25 payment (about $256 today) from William Everman of Jefferson Township, who later reported the men to the state police.

"The two men had approached Everman, representing themselves to be deputy sheriffs, and promised that they would refrain from prosecuting him, or prevent him from being molested if he desired to sell liquor, if he would give them $25."

All that said, one might ask where the tavern at the Mine Hill Hotel might have obtained the now-legally-prohibited booze to serve to its thirsty customers. Today locals speak anecdotally about bootleggers and rumrunners who frequented the area and were rumored to have hidden whiskey stills and booze shipments in the abandoned mines scattered throughout the area. And, indeed, the mines would have been ideal hiding places to stow away such contraband. Today the mine entrances have been completely sealed, but in the 1920s most were still open, though largely overgrown with plant life.

Again, *Daily Record* stories from the period give credence to tales of hidden stills. In December of 1925 a complete bottling plant with an estimated worth of $50,000 (about $500,000 today) was seized in a private garage of a Morris Plains estate. During the following year, a 250-gallon still, "in full operation," was found in Port Morris.

Also in 1926, a murder investigation that police believed was tied to a "bootlegging feud" led to the discovery of "one of the largest stills ever found in this county." The 2,600-gallon still, found in East Hanover, had the capacity to manufacture a gallon of hootch a minute. The area in which the still was found, the newspaper reported, "was an isolated one, although good roads lead by the door." The same description could just as easily be applied to the abandoned mine areas of Northern New Jersey.

Booze may not have been the only suspicious items hidden away in the now-vacant chambers of the Dickerson, Byram, Crane and Baker Mines, however. In 1991, the noted chemist Dr. William C. Zeek wrote an article for *Matrix*, a journal of the history of minerals, in which he described his childhood growing up in the Mine Hill of the 1920s. For several years, Zeek had been written up *in American Men & Women of Science*, a biographical directory of leaders in physical, biological, and related sciences, and he was in his early seventies when he wrote "Memories of Mine Hill" for *Matrix*.

In the story he describes how, after his mother passed away in 1926, he was taken to live with his maternal grandparents in Mine Hill. William A. Kinny, Zeek's grandfather, was gardener and caretaker for the estate of Frederick A. Canfield, a man who had some familiarity with the Mine Hill Hotel[1]. Canfield was also a highly respected mineral collector and great-nephew of the late Mahlon Dickerson, earlier mentioned as the town's most important historical figure and one time owner of the Dickerson Mine.

"During prohibition," Zeek wrote, "it was rumored that a number of the abandoned mines in the area were used by some of the gangs to dispose of the bodies of competitors. The Dickerson Mine pond and the echo shaft would have been ideal for such a purpose. I remember seeing cars going slowly past my grandfather's home late at night and returning in ten minutes or so, going as fast as the dirt road would permit. No bodies were ever found but no one really looked. A thug named 'Waxey' Gordon controlled the booze in the area. He was not a man who liked nosy people."

Waxey Gordon, born Irving Wexler, was indeed a dangerous and powerful man during the period. Rising up the ranks from pickpocket and street gangster (where he was known to break a jaw, an arm or even take a life if the situation called for it) to the top of the New York underworld, Gordon controlled a vast flow of booze that came into America through the New York and New Jersey coastlines. During the latter part of the 1920s, Gordon operated a host of breweries, which were officially licensed to sell "near beer" but which were really fronts to distribute the real stuff.

---

[1] *See page 29*

"By 1930, thanks to Eureka [Cereal Beverage Company, a brewery] and his other companies, Waxey was supplying beer to much of northern New Jersey and eastern Pennsylvania," wrote Albert Fried in "The Rise and Fall of the Jewish Gangster in America." "In that year alone, according to government accountants, he earned $1,427,531.42 on which, incidentally, he paid a grand total of $10 in taxes. And by then he had deposited over two million dollars in New Jersey banks, this apart from the cash he kept under personal lock and key."

Gordon was finally indicted for income tax evasion in 1933, thanks to rival gangsters Lucky Luciano and Meyer Lansky, who conspired to eliminate Waxey by secretly supplying the feds with incriminating information on him. When he got out of jail in 1940, dead broke and deeply in debt to the government, he promptly went back to a life of crime. In 1951 he was busted for heroin sales and sent to Alcatraz, where he died three years later, aged 66. But before his long, precipitous fall, Waxey Gordon spent over ten years as one of the most powerful mob figures in America, and was the head of the organization that likely supplied booze to the two local taverns in the little town of Mine Hill, N.J.

It had been clear to many, very early on, that prohibition just wasn't working. One of those was Ira Reeves—New Jersey's top prohibition enforcer—who, after only eight months on the job, realized it was impossible to put a cork in the liquor trade.

"He concluded that his work had been a failure; that all he had managed to do after countless raids and arrests was to raise the price and lower the quality of alcohol in the state," wrote "Jerseyana" author Marc Mappen of Reeves.

Reeves wasn't alone in his views. As early as 1920, Dover Mayor William L.R. Lynd was quoted in the *Jerseyman* as saying, "The police are helpless in the matter [of the dry law] and perhaps they have been indifferent, as men have been staggering through our streets and they have been getting drunk in Dover."

The same year, officials of Ottawa, Ontario, Canada released a summary opinion that efforts to stop the smuggling of liquor over the border to the United States were practically futile.

The Associated Press paraphrased the Ottawa law enforcement community thusly: "As long as profits from bootlegging are what they are, and the only deterrent is a fine of $200 or so, there will be big money in the bootlegging game and it will be very difficult for the authorities on either side of the international line to stamp out traffic."

Just after Christmas of 1926, the Assistant U.S. Attorney for the state of New York resigned from his post, declaring that prohibition "cannot be enforced in its present form."

By 1933 that was clear to just about everyone. It must have been an enormous relief to the owners of the Mine Hill Hotel when prohibition finally staggered to an end that year. Now their daily operations would no longer have included negotiations with mobsters, aggressive prohibition officials, cops-on-the-make, and the local temperance union, which was also quite active in town.

By the time prohibition was repealed, the second generation of the Glass family had taken over responsibility for the Mine Hill Hotel, though the actual ownership of the property was under dispute for several years. The trouble seems to have begun upon the death of David Glass on September 20, 1928. Technically David's sons Arthur (or Art) and Samuel were the executors of his estate. But the Glass boys renounced their executorships in respect to their mother, Augusta, who retained authority over her late husband's holdings.

However Augusta herself died less than a year later, on August 2, 1929. At that time Art Glass lived in Flushing, Long Island, though the rest of the family—consisting of the late David and Augusta's sons Samuel and Isadore; daughter and son-in-law Hattie and Joseph Bergenbach; and the late couple's various grandchildren—seem to have remained either at the family home on Sussex Street or elsewhere in the Dover area. Another daughter, Mamie Glass-Huber, pre-deceased David and Augusta, leaving three children of her own behind. Another son, Alexander, was a resident of the Greystone Park psychiatric facility in Morris Plains.

Prior to her death, Augusta signed a document purported to be her will, dated May 13, 1929, with Art and another man, Emil Heller, listed as executors. But the will was immediately challenged in court by Isadore Glass, who as a requirement of the will was ordered to repay a loan in the amount of $7,000 (the equivalent of about $73,400 today) to the Augusta Glass estate.

73

Isadore's contesting of the will sent it into Orphan's Court for review, and before long several other individuals stepped forward to claim a portion of the Glass estate, valued to be as much as $42,000, or about $440,500 today. As many as 29 claimants—from family members to business associates like Isadore Less (a realtor and property manager) to the Congregation of Adath Israel put in for a portion of the Glass thousands.

As a result, literally hundreds of court documents were filed between 1929 and 1931 relating to the Augusta Glass estate. Currently on file in the Surrogate Court of Morris County are close to 450 court documents on the matter, stored in microfiche.

A lay reading of these documents reveals an estate in disarray. According an affidavit signed by the executors of the challenged will, for example, Emil Heller and Arthur Glass "entered upon their duties in administering the estate, which duties were very arduous, due to the fact that the bulk of the estate consisted of real estate in a very bad and dilapidated condition. Your executors had considerable trouble keeping the same rented, keeping the properties in repair…They were also compelled to institute numerous suits in the District Court, for possession of premises or to recover rent."

While Isadore's claims against the estate were wrapped up fairly quickly by the Glass siblings, it took what appears to be hundreds of hours of work by the Glass family, attorneys and accountants to settle other outstanding issues of the estate. Augusta Glass had owned seventeen parcels of property in Dover, Rockaway and Mine Hill, all of which generated rental income which needed to either be disbursed to heirs or the properties sold outright, and only to the agreement of all concerned.

It appears from court documents that the rental income from the Mine Hill Hotel was only $40 in 1929, or about $430 today, suggesting the property was either vacant for several months during the period or that the tenants of the property were negligent in their payments. For the sake of comparison, another Glass property on West Blackwell Street in Dover brought in rental income of $2,421 for the same period, an astounding sum in Depression-era America, and the equivalent of about $25,400 today.

It's not clear who, precisely, was leasing the Mine Hill Hotel from the Glass family at the time. However several longtime Mine

Hill residents have colorful childhood memories of one woman they associated with the place. Either a barmaid or the manager of the property, "Big Mary" was a large woman of Eastern European descent who in the summer would walk over to Jackson Brook with her little poodle for a bath.

"She used to bathe in Granny's Brook," Abbie Ebner said. "Some people refer to it as Jackson Brook, which is the name you'd find on a map, but we always called it Granny's Brook. She'd walk down across a vacant field and go there on a summer afternoon and bathe. A lot of people did that. She had no indoor bathroom. No one did. We didn't, either. As kids we were always roaming the woods, and—after we were on to her habits—some of us would wait for her and call out to tease her when she was bathing. Then she'd hurry out of the water and get her clothes on or cover herself. Because she was totally naked with her when she was doing it. The water was not even knee deep."

Two or three other longtime locals—all now in their seventies or eighties—have vivid childhood memories of the sight of "Big Mary" and her dog down at Granny's Brook. All connect "Big Mary" to the tavern at the Mine Hill Hotel, but none could furnish any additional information about the zaftig barmaid and her little poodle. So for now, at least, "Big Mary" remains in the misty realm of a few seniors' youthful recollections.

When all was said and done, the Mine Hill Hotel ended up under the ownership of Glass siblings Art, Isadore, Samuel and Hattie—plus Hattie's husband Joseph Bergenbach—through much of the 1930s. In 1936, a fortyish woman from Dover began tending bar at the tavern of the property. Her name was Sadie Amato, and she was romantically involved with 47-year-old Art, who had moved back into the area.

Two years later, in 1938, Art decided to strike out on his own, purchasing the hotel from the other five beneficiaries of the Augusta Glass estate and installing Sadie at the bar for the duration.

CHAPTER SIX

Art & Sadie

Just off of Quaker Bridge Road in old Mount Fern, a couple of miles east of the Mine Hill Hotel, lies a cemetery in an old churchyard. Search long enough in this graveyard and you'll come across two stones of the same size, lying side by side. This is the last resting-place of Art Glass and Sadie Amato. Largely overlooked today, Amato's grave is partially obscured by shrubbery. Neither appears to have been visited in quite some time, as no flowers or plants adorn the spot.

Below Art Glass's name is the phrase, "Gone but not forgotten."

More than half a century after Art Glass shook loose his mortal coils, a dozen or so area residents still remember him vividly. Some of these folk were in poor health or were simply too old to talk at any length about Art and Sadie. Others were simply unwilling or uninterested. But there were some that were able to provide a colorful glimpse into life at the old Mine Hill Tavern under the proprietorship of Art Glass and Sadie Amato.

"There was a Jewish fella named Art Glass, he owned the place for a long time during the war years," Lifelong Mine Hill resident Albert "Abbie" Ebner said when asked of his earliest recollections of the Mine Hill Tavern. "He had a wood burning stove in the bar room. There was no restaurant there, it was only a bar. When Art Glass had it, it was a thriving business because of the war. A lot of men went there, servicemen, and they'd have parties there. My brother, who died of—among other things—alcoholism and cigarettes, frequented Art Glass's place. He was one of their best customers. Art was an affable fella. Very likeable."

Another longtime Mine Hill resident, Francis Burdge, also recalls the bar during this period. Burdge said Glass and Amato started the business modestly, with a single case of beer and a single case of soda. The hotel portion of the property was no longer in operation. The couple ran the business strictly as a bar, and kept the amenities simple.

"There was nothing modern in the place in any respect," Burdge said. "Art and Sadie used to go down to Dalrymple's Ice House to get a 300 pound block of ice to keep the beer cold. Art would sing and play the piano. He was the entertainment. He'd make up his own songs about the place, like '45 Miles From Broadway.'"

Other longtime residents remember that quality about Glass as well, even recalling some of the lyrics to Glass's more popular numbers, and pointing out that the tavern was then informally known as the "Green Hotel" or the "Green Room." It was given this distinction because Art would sometimes honor servicemen by switching on a light fixture with a green lightbulb, bathing the tavern in green light. When the green light was on, drinks for soldiers were "on the house." Glass especially liked to offer free drinks to servicemen who were either just heading out to the frontlines or just returning home from the war.

"45 miles from Broadway," Glass would sing, "Art Glass's Green Room Cafe." This was presumably in parody of George M. Cohan's "Forty Five Minutes From Broadway," the title song of the popular stage musical and a hit record for the pop singer Billy Murray in 1906.

"My grandfather used to sing," said Art Glass's granddaughter, Patricia Carper, who was a small child when her grandfather operated the Mine Hill Tavern. She now resides just a few doors down from the former Mine Hill Tavern, on West Randolph Ave. "I remember he had an old green rocking chair that he would sit in there in the bar room. He had these old tables, you know, with the wire backs on the chairs? Like tables at an old ice cream parlor."

80-year-old Helen Turpack first started going to the Mine Hill Tavern in 1939, at age 17, after moving to the area from Pennsylvania.

"When the jukebox played, Art would sing," Turpack said. "He had a megaphone. He'd say, 'Come to Art Glass's Green Room and have a good time! The heart of Mine Hill!' Well, everybody did come and everybody had a good time. It would get crowded. It was a little place, so when I say it was crowded, if you put 15 people in there it would get crowded, elbow to elbow.

"Art and Sadie were there all of time," she added. "I'd go there Friday and Saturday evenings, for music and dancing, not to drink. I had two brothers who worked at the Scrub Oaks mine, and we all used to go out there together. That was our recreation, because they worked all week. I was 17. I didn't know anybody. No boyfriends, nothing like that. I was just glad to go out and dance. We'd play that jukebox all night."

Turpack said that dancing at the tavern was something of a challenge, because there was no dance floor to speak of. Additionally, there were small tables scattered about the small bar area and steel posts positioned throughout the bar to support the ceiling.

"We'd dance right there at the bar, between the tables. Of course, you had these metal columns, and they were in your way, too, so you danced around them, too. We did plenty of polkas. Art made sure we had everything. We had a really good time there. And there was Nick Hryor, old Nick. He was a steady customer. Best customer there. He came there every night with his wife and had a few beers. He was a dancer, but not her. She sat at the bar and that was it. She never moved."

Hryor was an automobile mechanic who apparently spent every waking hour at the Mine Hill Tavern when he wasn't fixing cars at his garage on Thomastown Road. He'd show up at the bar in his work clothes—always stained with prodigious amounts of motor oil—and do his best to charm the ladies onto the dance floor. A lively, energetic man with a large, quiet Russian wife, he is still fondly remembered by many townsfolk.

"Nick danced with any one of us who would dance with him," Turpack said. "When the ladies had a few drinks, a few beers, they would dance with him. Mostly people drank beer, because that's what they could afford. It was cheap. I think it was a dime for a glass of beer. Old Nick was a jolly old guy. I can still see him dancing around those poles like crazy, I tell ya. He enjoyed it. We all did."

Longtime Mine Hill resident Everett Clark also remembers Hryor well.

"Old Nick used to bring his wife in and sit her down at the bar and then dance around like a monkey," he said. "He'd grab one of those poles and swing around and slide down them. He was quite a character. Always had a crew cut and wore suspenders. He always looked greasy because he was a mechanic."

Being a workingman's bar, one has to wonder if things ever got out of hand. Asked if there were ever brawls in the bar, Burdge said, "We heard arguments. Once in a while you'd walk by and somebody would start a fight and then Art and Sadie would flag them."

"It didn't get too rowdy," Clark said. "If somebody said something out of line, it would sometimes set people off, and it would threaten to get rowdy in a hurry. But then Art or Sadie would put you out. They didn't put up with it. I remember I walked in there one day, and I tripped in the doorway, in what we used to call the saddle. 'No more for you!' Sadie yelled. 'You're out!' She wouldn't give me a drink. So we never did get a drink that day."

Added Turpack, "I don't remember too many fights. If they got rowdy, Art got rid of 'em. He'd throw 'em out. He didn't take no bologna like that. He was a good guy. The men who were his customers were making something like fifty cents an hour in the mines. And Art was good to them. He took care of them and worried about them."

"Art was a big man," Burdge said. "Sadie was on the heavy side, too, but not really fat. Neither was very tall. I don't think they ever did get married."

At least two Mine Hill locals remember Sadie for her rather eccentric habit of driving her 1932 Chevrolet from the right-hand side of the front seat, almost as far to the right as a front seat passenger might sit. No Mine Hill resident who was interviewed for this book seems to have any idea why Sadie drove her signature vehicle in such an odd manner. Many simply smiled and shrugged it off as a picturesque oddity of small town life. But the amusing sight of Sadie Amato driving her antique auto to and from Dalrymple's with an enormous chunk of ice on the back of her car—and always driving from the right hand side—became a rather beloved routine in town, one that would be sadly missed when Sadie and her famous 1932 Chevy were no longer seen roaming the back roads of Mine Hill, NJ.

Francis Burdge was below the legal drinking age when Art and Sadie operated the tavern, but he lived just a few doors down from the place, and on Saturday nights in the summer he would stand outside one of the tavern windows and listen to Art sing: "That was our big entertainment on a Saturday night," he said.

Longtime area resident Bill Hunter said his father used to deliver Shaeffer beer to the tavern in the 1940s: "That's what they had on tap there," Hunter said. "Schaeffer and Rheingold."

Hunter also remembers the old Wurlitzer-style jukebox, located at one end of the bar, just before the entrance to the men's room. "The jukebox was one of the old kind with an arm that would swing around and picked the record up. Then the record comes down onto the turntable. It played all old stuff. This was the 1940s. Tommy Dorsey, Ray Anthony, Glen Miller. The jukebox was over by the men's room, which was terrible. It stunk to high heaven. Oh, my god. There was a men's urinal at the end of the bar, on the right hand side. But it was only as big as a phone booth. You couldn't take your wiener out and walk in the door at the same time. That's how small it was. You had to wait to get situated to get it out."

Turpack recalled that the ladies' room was upstairs on the second floor, while the mens' room, with its trough-style urinal, was located approximately where Hunter recalled it to be.

"The ladies' bathroom was upstairs," she said. "It was an ordinary bathroom, like you'd see in someone's home, with a tub and a sink and commode. That's where you went. With all of the customers you'd have to wait on line to get into the bathroom. But of course the men...you know how men are. If there was a line for the mens' room, they'd go outside. It was all woodsy. You know, all grown-in. The men drank a lot of beer, but they did alright."

Another longtime area resident said she also remembered an upstairs ladies' room, just above the bar. And, she said, when there were plumbing problems—as there often are in extremely old houses—sometimes the toilet would overflow and leak directly onto the bar below.

Talk about having "a little something extra" in your cocktail!

Hunter said the crowd at the bar was largely made up of farmers, miners and hunters, and the area surrounding the tavern was thickly forested.

"It was a shady, shady place," Hunter said with a laugh.

Like many old-time country bars, the Mine Hill Tavern was heated with an old wood stove in one corner of the property. Ebner remembers that the stove was fueled with cast-off wood from a local lumber mill.

"Art Glass fueled his wood-burning stove with slab lumber, and one day he bought a truckload of it to fuel his stove," Ebner said. "I got in on this job [of cutting up the slab wood for Glass] with my brother and one of his buddies. My brother Harold was out of work a good part of the time during the early 1940s. Because he was alcoholic, he'd get a good job and then he'd screw it up. He worked at Allen Wood Steel Company's Scrub Oaks Mine. Bill Shaw, my brother's friend, was also an alcoholic. So the three of us went to the tavern and a saw was set up there. We worked on cutting up the wood for Art's stove for a good part of the day. Afterward Harold and Bill went inside and spent a good deal of the money they made drinking. I don't know that I earned anything at all that day. I loved my brother so much that my participation was probably a gratis thing on my part."

In 1940, Ebner was only 15 years old, so he wasn't served liquor when he went to the Mine Hill Tavern.

"When my brother was ready to go into the service, he was 35 years old, which is old for the draft. Anyway, Harold was so well-liked that his friends had a half a dozen going-away parties for him, one of which was at Art Glass's tavern, which was very well attended and was a good time."

Less of a good time was another incident involving Ebner's brother Harold, Abbie recounted.

"My brother was on maneuvers in Tennessee, and on one of his furloughs he came home. The way you traveled then was by train or Greyhound bus. My brother was scheduled to go back. His furlough was over. But he wasn't showing up to get his bus. Because I loved him, I remember going to Art Glass's, knowing that Harold would be there, getting bombed. Because he had a big affection for me, too, I thought I might be able to convince him to go back to Tennessee.

"I remember sitting next to him at the bar. He was very good-looking so there were always women around, and they were there that day, too, sitting next to him at the bar. I remember pleading with him to get on the bus to go back to Tennessee. And he finally did. He listened to me, even though he was much older than I. He got back to the base late, though, and ended up peeling potatoes for a long time afterward."

Where there is booze, there is inevitably sex, and the tavern at the Mine Hill Hotel was no exception, according to Ebner.

"My wife and I had very close friends who were about twenty years our senior, Jim and Marian Gainer. Jim was a colorful personality. He had been in the Marines and was just a little cocky little Irishman. He grew up in Brooklyn and was a wiseass but a love bug. He was a guard at Picatinny [arsenal, in nearby Rockaway Township]. He used to entertain me with a lot of colorful stories about what he did as a young man during the 1930s.

"In those days there was no banister on the second floor walkway of the tavern. Jim claimed that he was making love to some woman on that walkway. They became so engrossed in their activities that they rolled off onto the ground below. Neither of them was hurt. Probably both of them bounced."

The fun at the tavern continued through the war, and was no doubt the site of many victory drinks when World War II came to an end in 1945. By that time the little tavern was thriving.

"They started investing more and more into the place, till they could really get it started," Burdge said. "My father used to frequent the bar then, and a guy named Ernie Pickle was a fixture there. He was always in there when he wasn't at home."

By the mid-1940s, Art's two children by his previous wife, Irene, were a regular presence at the tavern. Marguerite Glass-Andrews and Russell Glass were the third generation of the Glass family to become involved in the bar's operation.

Through the war years Marguerite had been married to Ira Andrews, an employee of Picatinny Arsenal, with whom she had two daughters, Patricia and Bernice. But on Halloween, 1945—when Patricia was eight years old and Bernice three—Ira left his little family for a woman he had met at work, Adele Szarka. According to Bernice "Bea" Hickler, the younger of Marguerite's two daughters, Ira remained a semi-regular presence in his daughters lives from that point forward, visiting the family in Mine Hill a couple of times a year and paying a small amount of child support.

"After that my mother worked cleaning houses, and on weekends my Uncle Russell would pick up my mother and take her to the tavern, where she worked for my grandfather," Hickler recounted via email from her home in Pennsylvania. Hickler also speculated that Russell likely worked at the tavern. He resided in Morristown at the time and wouldn't have likely driven from Morristown to his family home in Wharton—where Marguerite resided—simply to provide a ride to work for his sister, she said.

"My uncle probably did work at the tavern sometimes with my mother if he didn't have a date," Hickler wrote via email. "I don't think he would drive up to Wharton from Morristown just to take my mother to work. I don't think people did a lot of driving back then."

Like many siblings, the Glass kids occasionally had spats, Hickler said.

"One night my uncle and mother got into an argument and he wouldn't take my mother home," Hickler wrote. "John Babisky was at the tavern and he offered to bring my mother home, and that was the start of their relationship. I don't know how long my mother worked at the tavern, but I know she knew Sadie."

Babisky—a World War II veteran and employee of Hercules Power Works in Kenvil—courted Marguerite for over two decades before the couple were married in 1968. They remained together happily until Marguerite's death from a heart ailment in November of 1992.

With the collapse of Marguerite's marriage and the struggle to raise two small daughters alone, the mid-1940s must have been a very difficult time. Unfortunately the young woman would have to endure yet another blow. In 1946 her father died, leaving much of his property to Amato.

"I hereby give and bequeath unto the said Sadie M. Amato, the business now operated by me at Mine Hill, New Jersey, and known as the Mine Hill Tavern," he wrote in his will, "including the good will thereof, all personal property used in connection therewith and all monies that may be on hand in said tavern at the time of my decease together with all money which shall be on deposit in any bank or trust company in the joint names of myself and the said Sadie M. Amato, my jewelry, household furnishings, wearing apparel and personal belongings."

The remainder of Art Glass's estate was left to Russell and Marguerite. Further, he stipulated that "after the death of Sadie Amato, or after she shall dispose of or sell [the Mine Hill Tavern], or shall discontinue the operation of said business, then and in such case I hereby give and devise the same unto my son, Russell Glass and my daughter, Marguerite Andrews…"

Because of this condition of the will, the deed for the Mine Hill Tavern remained in the hands of Art Glass's children until such time as Sadie Amato decided to dispose of the property. In the 1960s, when the property was finally sold again, it was the surviving child of Art Glass, rather than Sadie Amato herself, who signed over the deed to the next owner.

"Sadie had lifetime rights to the property," Pat Carper said.

Sadly, it wasn't long before another death darkened the lives of the Glass family. Four years after Art Glass's death, on July 9, 1950, 34-year-old Russell Glass drowned in Cozy Lake in Jefferson Township. The Glass family had come to the lake to visit one of Marguerite's relatives, George Anderson. Police said Russell had been wading in the lake when he went under. Oddly, the lake was shallow all the way across except for one spot near a dock that had been dredged out the previous winter. Russell, who apparently couldn't swim, unfortunately found himself in exactly that spot.

Local children said they saw him "bob up and down several times" when he disappeared without making a sound. The children called for help, some swimmers fished him from the lake, and rescue workers tried for two hours to revive him, to no avail.

"We had taken Uncle Russ over from one shore to another by rowboat," Carper recalled. "Then we returned to the other side of the lake to visit my grandmother. By the time we got back to the beach where we left him, he had gone in the water—I don't know why he did that, because he couldn't swim—and evidently there was a piling and he fell down into a hole. I was in the rowboat with Johnny—my stepfather—and by the time we had gotten back from across the lake Uncle Russ was drowned already. I don't know, exactly, what happened. It was hard to believe that that could happen in such a short time."

Hickler recalled that while Pat and the rest of the family were rowing across the lake to their grandmother's home, Hickler remained behind on the beach with her uncle. She had been playing at the beach when she saw a body being removed from the water.

"He was supposed to watch me as I was only eight years old," Hickler wrote via email. "Just before [the rest of the family] got back to the beach, I found out it was my uncle they had pulled from the water. This is something I will never forget."

Russell had been a World War II veteran, inducted into service Sept. 15, 1942 and served in the European area with the 446 Bomber Group of the Eighth Air Force. In 1950 the war was still fresh on the minds of most Americans, and the tragic, freak accident that took the life of Russell Glass briefly drew great attention and empathy from the citizens of Morris County. Much as the drowning death of Elizabeth Ellis had sixty years earlier, Russell's death was widely reported in the local papers.

The tremendous shock of Russell's death fundamentally affected the Glass family. Hickler said Russell "enjoyed life," and that "he had several girlfriends." His death was keenly felt, particularly by Art's former wife Irene, who seemed to favor her son.

"My grandmother had a bad heart...and they thought it would kill her when she found out that my uncle had drowned," Hickler wrote. "But she lived many years after."

From the late 1940s through the early 1960s, Sadie Amato operated the little bar on the corner of Randolph and West Randolph Avenues on her own. At a time when few women held full-time jobs and even fewer ran their own businesses, Sadie managed a successful tavern without the benefit of her companion, Art Glass, at her side. It wasn't always easy.

"Sadie was a character," said Vickie Campisi, who would occasionally visit the Mine Hill Tavern during the 1950s. "She was very tough. She'd throw people out if she needed to, and it was kind of a rough crowd. Miners and hunters were her customers. Most of the time they'd go there and get drunk and then they'd go out hunting. I don't know how they hunted like that. I know I wouldn't have wanted to be out in the woods then."

After a brief telephone interview in mid-2002, Campisi and her family declined further interview requests. She and her husband Joseph were lifelong friends of later tavern owner Madeline Bellini and her husband, Frank, who also occasionally drank at the tavern during the period.

Campisi described Sadie's Mine Hill Tavern—as it was then known—as "a bar of last resort" with sardine cans for ashtrays and spitoons lining the foot-rest railing that ran the length of the bar. A pot-bellied stove kept the place heated in the winter. Two huge, long-necked jars—one of pickled eggs, one of pickled pig's feet—shared the bar's surface with perpetual bowls of salted pretzels and peanuts.

Campisi and others confirmed one of the most colorful and persistent rumors of the Sadie's era. According to several Mine Hill Tavern regulars, Sadie is reported to have told several people that cowboy star George "Gabby" Hayes stopped by for a drink during the time she operated the tavern.

"Yes," Campisi said. "Gabby Hayes really did go there."

Hayes, the veteran of dozens of horse operas, radio shows and a successful NBC-TV program, was among the most popular western stars in Hollywood from the 1930s through his retirement in 1953. His grizzled old prospector character, with his signature long white whiskers, was sidekick to such western legends as John Wayne, Hopalong Cassidy and Roy Rogers.

But why would one of Hollywood's most popular personalities stop at an out-of-the-way New Jersey tavern while at the peak of his career? Several locals have their theories. For instance, Hayes could have been in the area to make a personal appearance at the Wild West City amusement park in nearby Netcong; or at the Playhouse Theater in Dover, which was known to show only western films; or he might have been staying at one of the grand hotels of nearby Mount Freedom in Randolph Township, which in the 1940s and 50s provided accommodations for entertainers like Frank Sinatra and Phil Silvers.

Others point out that a prominent plastic surgeon resided on Hurd Street in Mine Hill for many years, and played host to many of the Broadway and Hollywood stars for whom he provided occasional lifts and tucks. Jean Harlow, Betty Grable and Marlene Dietrich were all rumored to have been among this physician's patients, and all of whom were said to have spent part of their recovery period at his secluded rural home in Mine Hill. Given this surgeon's myriad show business contacts, it's certainly possible that he and Hayes were acquainted, and that during a visit to this doctor's home, Hayes stopped in for a drink at Sadie's.

Another intriguing theory involves the B-movie star Kirk Alyn, today most famous for portraying Superman in two movie serials in 1948 and 1950. Alyn, who lived in Wharton during his childhood, co-starred with Hayes in 1943's "Overland Mail Robbery," a B-western with "Wild Bill" Elliott in the lead role. It's possible that Alyn and Hayes became friendly during the course of filming and that Alyn invited Hayes to accompany him back to his hometown for a visit. During the course of their stay, this theory goes, they might have gone out for a drink in Mine Hill. Though Alyn was kind of a hometown hero—having appeared in small roles in films starring Fred Astaire, Abbott & Costello and Victor Mature—Gabby was the more recognizable name star and would have made a stronger impression on the local folks drinking in Sadie's that day.

Of course, there's always the possibility that Sadie could have been making the whole thing up. But those who knew her dismiss this out of hand. Sadie was a tough-minded woman not given to flights of fancy. If she said Gabby Hayes had been at her tavern, then he probably was.

"Sadie was there to make money," Ebner said. "She had a business. She wasn't fun loving. She was there to make a livelihood."

As the 1950s gave way to the 1960s, however, Sadie's health was reportedly starting to lag. She had suffered from a blood disease for several years, according to Burdge, and was constantly afraid of nicks and cuts that might endanger her health. Burdge said Amato had "sugar diabetes," but from his description of her ailment, it would seem that Sadie more likely suffered from some form of hemophilia, a bleeding disorder in which it can take a prolonged period of time for the blood to clot and abnormal bleeding can occur.

"If somebody broke a glass on the bar, she would flag them," Burdge said. "She was afraid of getting cut because she was afraid they wouldn't be able to stop the bleeding."

In 1961 she decided to give up her lifetime rights to the Mine Hill Tavern and on September 12 of that year, fun-loving couple

Frank and Madeline "Maddie" Bellini took over the tavern's operation.

The *News-Leader* of Netcong-Stanhope ran a page two item on Sadie's decision to sell the tavern. A photograph shows Sadie (in cat-glasses and an old-fashioned dark dress with lace fringe at the neck) shaking hands with Frank Bellini, a tall, robust looking man with a broad smile and a short-sleeved knit shirt. The caption reads:

"YEARS AND YEARS—Mrs. Sadie Amato at the door of her 1932 Chevrolet wishes Frank Bellini well. He just finished buying the Mine Hill Inn from her. Mrs. Amato is retiring after 25 years and will tour the South in her auto. The popular tavern at the intersection of Randolph Avenue and Quaker Church Road in Mine Hill got that way by continuing a policy of selling a glass of beer for ten cents, a cheerful note in these inflated times."

The caption got a few small details wrong. Sadie didn't actually sell the tavern to the Bellinis, for example. Marguerite Glass-Andrews, the holder of the deed on the property, was the seller. Additionally, it appears that Frank and Madeline Bellini leased the property from Marguerite for a couple of years before purchasing the property outright. The deed for the sale of the tavern to the Bellinis is dated August 1, 1963. Also, the cross streets upon which the tavern is located are inaccurately described in the newspaper.

A few months later, Frank and Maddie took out an advertisement in *News-Leader* to announce their official grand opening. It was to be held November 18, 1961 at 10 p.m. Carl "Butch" Gladish, Frank and Madeline's nephew and occasional bartender, remembers those early days of the Bellini's ownership of the tavern well.

"My aunt and uncle bought the place in 1961," Gladish said. "When they bought it, it had a dirt floor, it had spitoons, outdoor bathrooms. They didn't have decent indoor bathrooms. So my uncle put in new bathrooms and put the wooden floor down. That floor, I don't know how many times I had to patch it up because it would start rotting. My Uncle Frank put in two-by-ten flooring right on top of the ground."

"It was the last place to have ten cent beers for the longest time," Gladish added. "The woman who had it before them was Sadie Amato. She used to have an old antique car with a big metal grate on the back that she'd use to bring the ice back and forth."

Prior to purchasing the tavern, Gladish said, the Bellinis owned three area gas stations. Asked why they decided to buy Sadie's tavern, Gladish said, "They used to like to drink. They used to like to party. Even when I was a kid, I remember they used to have parties in our basement. I remember my Uncle Frank bringing home pizzas. We used to sneak downstairs and watch them party when we were kids."

Charles "Chuck" O'Neill was a bartender and friend of Madeline Bellini during the last five or ten years of her life. He said that Madeline once told him a fascinating story about the day she first moved into the tavern with Frank.

"Maddie said that on the day Sadie moved out of the place, Sadie had a friend helping her, and the two women were carrying out shoeboxes from the attic," Chuck recounted. "Maddie asked Sadie if she needed help, and Sadie said, 'No, I don't need help.' They were loading everything into an old car, like a Model-T or something, Then the woman who was helping Sadie dropped one of the shoeboxes while she was on her way out to the car, and all of this money spilled out of it. Maddie estimated that if all of those boxes were filled with money, Sadie must have had tens of thousands of dollars in those shoeboxes. She had never gone to a bank. She had all of her money in shoe boxes, in this room."

After her motor tour of the South in her little 1932 Chevrolet, Sadie returned to the area. She was residing on South Bergen Street in Dover when she died at Dover General Hospital on April 15, 1967. She was 71 years old and had been ill, probably with cancer, for several years. She left no survivors. In her will, Sadie left everything to a Dover resident named Jennie Radmore, who was presumably the recipient of that famous 1932 Chevy and various shoeboxes of money. Radmore herself died in 1991.

During the final days of Sadie's life, Madeline Bellini paid her a visit, according to O'Neill. Unfortunately the once vibrant Amato was now a shadow of her former self and had difficulty recognizing her old acquaintance.

"Years later Maddie found Sadie in a hospital in Dover," O'Neill said. "Apparently she had nothing left. She was sitting there in a wheelchair and she barely knew who Maddie was. It was very sad."

PRELUDE TO PART II

Friday, January 20, 1995 was a poignant anniversary for Madeline "Maddie" Bellini. On that date in 1993 she had lost one of the most important people in her life, and two years later she had not yet completely gotten over her grief. Now residing in a doublewide trailer home owned by her sister, Jean Rose Sharp, Maddie's thoughts constantly went back to her happy days as the proprietor of the Mine Hill Tavern. She had sold the property just three months previous, and while she seemed to be enjoying her new retirement in Citra, Florida, some of her friends noticed that a little of her old spark was gone.

"She was so brokenhearted that Friday," recalled a friend who had spent that January day with Maddie and Jeanie in 1995. "I had made a clock for her with a picture of the old Mine Hill Tavern as its face. She asked me to hang it on the wall. She had tears in her eyes when she said, 'Bless my sweet tavern and all of the people within.'"

The two sisters and their friend from New Jersey put away quite a few drinks that day, some in toasts to the tavern and her old acquaintances back in Mine Hill. They went to a local bar and spent a good part of the day there. Around dinnertime the little trio decided to get a bite to eat.

"We were over there [at the bar] at about 5:30," their friend recounted. "Maddie's sister Jeanie said, 'Come on, Maddie. I've got food at home.' And Maddie said, 'No, I want to go to Luigi's.' We went down Route 441, which was right in front of the bar."

Luigi's was a popular Italian restaurant in the Ocala area. The friend from New Jersey was scheduled to fly home early on Sunday, and Maddie apparently wanted to treat him to dinner before he left. That she was pretty drunk at the time she got behind the wheel of the car was of little concern to Jeanie or Maddie's old friend. They had seen her drive quite well while intoxicated before.

"Maddie was the best drunk driver I ever saw," recalled Chuck O'Neill, another old friend and former employee, years later.

On her way out of the bar, Maddie passed an elderly gentleman who was whittling souvenirs for the tourists. She stopped a moment and gave him a couple of dollars for a small trinket.

"He had whittled these little key chains," the friend from New Jersey said. "So Maddie bought one and gave me this little key chain with a white dove on it, flying. She said, 'Here's something to remember me by.' She gave me that before we got in the car that afternoon."

Back in New Jersey, one former Maddie's Mine Hill Tavern regular, 27-year-old Molly Chapel, was attending a party when she suddenly realized that January 20 was an important date for both Maddie and the old crowd at the tavern. She called a few friends together and offered a toast.

"That day a very good friend of mine celebrated her 30th birthday," Molly said. "And I knew about the anniversary. So we had a drink to Maddie that night. In fact, later on that night, somebody found me to tell me what had happened down in Florida that day. It freaked me out a little because we had just drank to them a couple of hours earlier."

At 5:50 p.m., Maddie maneuvered her big, boxy 1991 Buick onto a paved median in the center of Route 441 and prepared to make a left turn into the driveway of Luigi's. Her blood alcohol content was an astounding .25. Beside her in the front seat was her friend from New Jersey. In the back seat was her sister Jean.

"I can't explain what happened next," her friend said. "It was unreal. It wasn't quite dark yet and there were lights further down the road."

Eddie Hendricks was an old friend who had briefly worked as a bartender at Maddie's Mine Hill Tavern in the months before Maddie sold the place. In the early evening of January 20, 1995, Hendricks suddenly got the urge to pick up the phone. He called Jeanie Sharp's doublewide trailer, deciding that he needed to talk to his old friend Maddie.

The phone rang and rang. There was no answer.

Maddie's car entered the northbound inside lane of Route 441 and continued across through the outside lane. Already traveling north on the highway was a 1993 Ford driven by Michael Kevin Kelly of Ocala.

"She went to turn the car," her friend from New Jersey said. "and I turned back to say something to Jeanie, and a streak of light came across the corner of my eye. I knew we were going to get hit, and we did."

Both cars spun out after the impact. The Ford ended up facing southeast, halfway in the northbound outside lane and partly in the driveway to Luigi's. The Buick came to a rest in a ditch on the east side of the road.

Paramedics arrived at the scene at 5:58 p.m.

Maddie was declared dead at 6:07.

She had spent nearly half her life behind the bar at her little tavern in Mine Hill, NJ. When those 33 years were over, the end came very, very quickly.

The earliest known exterior photo of the Mine Hill Hotel, taken between 1902 and 1911, when former East Stroudsburg, Penn. residents Austin and Louisa Treible owned the property.

A group of turn-of-the-century gentlemen (with a few small
children) gather on the exterior railed walkway of the Mine Hill
Hotel. Many of these men are believed to be out of work miners.
Locals speculate that the man at the center of the photo holding a
baby is Austin Treible.

The Mine Hotel is believed to have been a stagecoach stop. Stages like the one shown above, from a 1923 *Newark Evening News* article, would have transported passengers from the rail station in Dover to nearby Succasunna, possibly with a stop in Mine Hill along the way.

The tavern at the Mine Hill Hotel was always known as a miner's bar, and the several of the gentlemen in the photos on this page, and the following two, were likely to have been regular customers at the tavern. They show gatherings of "The Down and Out Club," believed to be a social group of out-of-work miners. (From the Morrissey Collection, courtesy of the Ferromonte Historical Society of Mine Hill)

"The Down and Out Club" was likely founded after 1902, when all but one of the 22 iron mines that dotted Mine Hill were shut down, leaving scores of men out of work. Several of these "Down and Out Club" members can also be seen in the group photo at the Mine Hill Hotel on page 97. (From the Morrissey Collection, courtesy of the Ferromonte Historical Society of Mine Hill)

One more "Down and Out Club" photo. Unfortunately none of
the men (or the rather blurry dog) in this photo can be
conclusively identified, but it's safe to say they enjoyed the
occasional beverage, as the bottles lined up on the front porch
attest. (From the Morrissey Collection, courtesy of the
Ferromonte Historical Society of Mine Hill)

ties. One or two of the religious societies have in operation machinery for extensive useful-ness.

The Moore Tragedy—Verdict of Murder in the Second Degree.

The trial of Solomon D. Moore was concluded yesterday in the Morris County Court of Oyer and Terminer. At the opening of the Court Mr. J. J. Cutler resumed the summing up for the defense, after which Attorney-General Gilchrist closed for the State. The charge of Judge Dalrimple was remarkable for its impartiality. In the course of its delivery he avoided all reference to the evidence, and confined his remarks to the law of the case. At the conclusion of the charge, about 4½ o'clock, the jury retired to consider their verdict, and at 8:44 o'clock it was announced they had agreed. After the usual preliminaries the foreman handed in a verdict of murder in the second degree. The Court stated that sentence would be pronounced next week. The prisoner did not exhibit any sign of emotion. Throughout the day the court-room was crowded to excess,

New York Times coverage of the trial of Solomon David Moore for the murder of his wife Mary Ann on Thanksgiving, 1872.

There will be a

REOPENING BALL,

given at the

MINE HILL HOTEL

FRIDAY, MAY 26, 1899.

There will be good music in attendance and accomodation for horses and wagons.

COME ONE   COME ALL

AND HAVE A GOOD TIME.

M. E. BEAM,

PROPRIETOR.

STANDARD JOE PRINT, DOVER, N.J.

A poster advertising the Mine Hill Hotel's grand reopening ball in 1899 (Courtesy of Barbara Spagna).

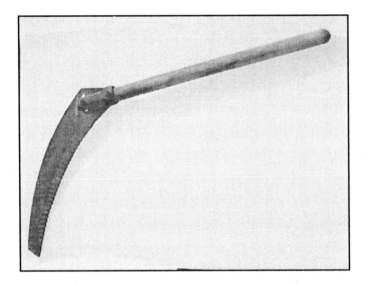

A corn hook similar to the one used in the 1886 murder of John Smith. This particular corn hook is currently on display at the Ferramonte Historical Society of Mine Hill's Bridget Smith House museum. (Photo by the author)

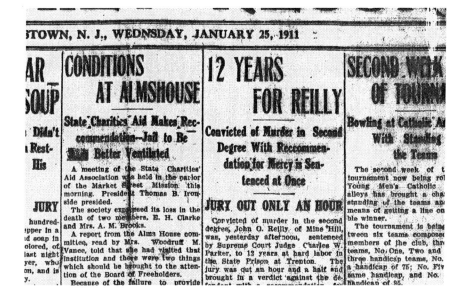

:TOWN, N. J., WEDNESDAY, JANUARY 25, 1911

CONDITIONS AT ALMSHOUSE

State Charities Aid Makes Recommendation--Jail to Be Made Better Ventilated

A meeting of the State Charities' Aid Association was held in the parlor of the Market Street Mission this morning. President Thomas B. Ironside presided.

The society expressed its loss in the death of two members, E. H. Clarke and Mrs. A. M. Brooks.

A report from the Alms House committee, read by Mrs. Woodruff M. Vance, told that she had visited that institution and there were two things which should be brought to the attention of the Board of Freeholders.

Because of the failure to provide

12 YEARS FOR REILLY

Convicted of Murder in Second Degree With Recommendation for Mercy is Sentenced at Once

JURY OUT ONLY AN HOUR

Convicted of murder in the second degree, John O. Reilly, of Mine Hill, was, yesterday afternoon, sentenced by Supreme Court Judge Charles W. Parker, to 12 years at hard labor in the State Prison at Trenton. The jury was out an hour and a half and brought in a verdict against the de...

SECOND WEEK OF TOURN...

Bowling at Catholic A... With Standing the Teams

The second week of t... tournament now being rol... Young Men's Catholic... alleys has brought a cha... standing of the teams an... means of getting a line on... ble winner.

The tournament is being... tween six teams composed... members of the club, thre... teams, No. One, Two and... three handicap teams, No. ... a handicap of 75; No. Fiv... same handicap, and No. ... handicap of 95.

The Morris County *Daily Record*'s coverage of the 1910 trial of John Reilly for the murder of Pat Gallagher.

Art Glass with his granddaughter Patricia in front of the Mine Hill Tavern, 1942. (Courtesy of Patricia Carper)

An unidentified man hoists a beer keg behind Art Glass. Glass is facing the front of the tavern, with his back to a parcel of land that is now the Cornelius House parking lot. (Courtesy of Patricia Carper)

Art with his daughter Marguerite standing behind the tavern in 1937. (Courtesy of Patricia Carper)

**Russell Glass sits astride his motorcycle in front of the tavern.
(Courtesy of Patricia Carper)**

**Art and Sadie Amato behind the bar at the Mine Hill Tavern,
probably late 1930s. (Courtesy of Patricia Carper)**

Mine Hill Tavern regular Harold Ebner at the time of his military service in World War II. (Courtesy of Albert Ebner)

Harold Ebner's teenage brother Abbie (above) once convinced Harold to return to his base rather than go AWOL and continue drinking at the popular bar. *(Courtesy of Albert Ebner)*

**The graves of Art Glass and Sadie Amato lie side by side at a
Randolph Township cemetery. (Photos by the author)**

YEARS AND YEARS — Mrs. Sadie Amato at door of her 1932 Chevrolet wishes Frank Bellini well. He just finished buying the Mine Hill Inn from her. Mrs. Amato is retiring after 25 years and will tour the South in her auto. The popular tavern at the intersection of Randolph Avenue and Quaker Church Road in Mine Hill got that way by continuing a policy of selling a glass of beer for ten cents, a cheerful note in these inflated times.

A newspaper photo celebrates the sale of the tavern to the Bellinis.

Marguerite Glass-Andrews as she looked in the early 1960s, when she sold the tavern to Frank and Madeline Bellini (courtesy of Bea Hickler).

Matt Connor

Madeline Bellini poses with Sadie behind the bar at the tavern.

**Popular cowboy film star Gabby Hayes is said to have stopped by
the Mine Hill Tavern for a drink during the Sadie's era.**

The Mine Hill Tavern as it appeared in the mid- to late-1950s, when it was operated solely by Sadie Amato. That's Sadie's famous 1932 Chevy parked in front of the building.

MADELINE and FRANK BELLINI
invite all to attend

OPEN HOUSE
Saturday, Nov. 18 10 p. m.
In Honor of Their

GRAND OPENING
- Krueger Ambassador Beer
- Buffet

MINE HILL TAVERN

Frank and Madeline Bellini advertise the grand opening of the Mine Hill Tavern in the Netcong-Stanhope *News-Leader*, 1961.

The Frank & Maddie's crowd in a photo dated September 16, 1967. Given the date, Maddie was likely celebrating her sixth anniversary as the tavern owner. Maddie is at center. Hazel Lapadula is to the left of Maddie.

Wooden nickels were redeemable for a free drink at Maddie's.

**Maddie with Ernie Pickle, a regular presence at the Mine Hill
Tavern for years. Marion Green sits at the bar behind them. She
would die tragically a few years later, the victim of a hit-and-run
accident.**

The handsome Frank Bellini before his death from cyrosis in 1969

**An unidentified woman poses with (from left) Hazel Lapadula,
Maddie and Marion Green in a 1967 photo.**

The petit, ladylike Kitty Stenkowitz often tended bar at the tavern. Here Kitty (center) poses with Maureen (left) and Maddie in a 1960s photo.

In the early 1960s, Maddie found companionship with Maureen Kavanaugh, whom her husband had hired as a barmaid.

Twenty eight years later Maddie and Maureen were still running the tavern together.

A Maddie's coaster

Dean Allan Ross, a talented artist and Maddie's regular who died far too young.

A Matchbook cover from the Frankie & Maddie era

Karl "Butch" Gladish tending bar in 1982.

Former dancer Harvey Klein serving drinks in 1985.

Maddie and Chuck O'Neill, 1994.

Michael Toussaint, Maddie and "Stephen Burns" in 1982

Maddie sometimes hosted drag shows, though not with any regularity. "Bobby" performs as Judy Garland's Dorothy from "The Wizard of Oz."

Michael Toussaint, a.k.a. "Michael Christopher" performs as Bette Midler. Note the ceiling with its multiple signatures.

Maddie and Maureen died two years apart to the day, in 1993 and '95. Patsy Cline's "Sweet Dreams" was among their favorite songs. (Photo by the author)

Maureen Kavanaugh had a tendency to smoke too much and imbibe a few too many, which eventually took their sad toll. Above is the Maureen many Mine Hill Tavern regulars remember today.

**Few, unfortunately, recall the vibrant young woman Maureen
once was.**

Maddie with old friend Lew Rothbart in October, 1994, just before she sold the bar and moved to Florida.

In one of Maddie's last photos, she relaxes in her sister Jeanie's double-wide trailer in December, 1994.

"Stephen Burns," Maddie, friend Andy Nease and Jeanie Sharp at the Grey Fox bar in Ocala in 1994. Weeks later, Maddie would leave this same bar en route to Luigi's restaurant when she would be killed in a horrendous car accident.

Exterior of Maddie's Mine Hill Tavern as it looked during the 1980s and early 1990s. (*Courtesy of the Historic Preservation Office, New Jersey Department of Environmental Protection***)**

Maddie's automobile after the accident that took her life.

In 1994, new owners Robert and Barbara Spagna undertook an ambitious renovation of the old Mine Hill Tavern. (Courtesy of Barbara Spagna)

During the renovations to the property, the Spagnas uncovered a wonderful folk art painting of the USS Maine under decades of paneling and wallpaper. (Courtesy of Barbara Spagna)

**The vastly altered interior of Cornelius House after the Spagnas
completed renovations. (Courtesy of Barbara Spagna)**

The property in the midst of ongoing exterior renovation.
(Courtesy of Barbara Spagna)

Cornelius House as it looks today.
(Photo by the author)

PART TWO
1961-2003
"This is it, MHT"

CHAPTER SEVEN

Undercover gay bar

At first, everything stayed pretty much the same at the Mine Hill Tavern. Folks who frequented the bar during the Sadie Amato era would have found that little had changed under the proprietorship of Frank and Madeline Bellini. The young couple was quite a bit more energetic and light-hearted than the elderly, all-business Amato, but the environment at the bar was largely unchanged, with regulars like Ernie Pickle practically living at the place and the Schaeffer and Reingold beer flowing like water.

One seemingly minor change, however, would be the catalyst for one of the most memorable characteristics of the Bellini period. On the day Frank and Maddie moved into the tavern, Frank took a narrow-tipped painter's brush and a can of orange paint and wrote the following phrase on the ceiling above the bar:

Frank-Madeline Bellini
September 12, 1961

It was a small gesture, really. A way to mark an important occasion in the couple's life. But it ended up launching an odd tradition that eventually became a trademark of the property. Noticing the Frank-Madeline inscription over the bar, customers began inscribing their own names in chalk on the ceiling of the little tavern.

Before long there were dozens of names chalked on the ceiling. By the seventies there were literally thousands of overlapping inscriptions. By the eighties, thousands more. By that time, the ceiling of the Mine Hill Tavern was a kind of a historical document. Almost everyone who passed through the doors of the bar left a little of himself or herself on that ceiling. If one searched long and hard enough by the time the Mine Hill Tavern closed in the mid-1990s, one could find the names of individuals who had come and gone decades earlier, who might be completely forgotten but for a few scribbled words on the ceiling of a little bar.

Bar patrons Ev and Marge[2] first started going to the Mine Hill Tavern in the 1970s. Marge wasn't crazy about the joint, but Ev liked it right away.

"I went in there and I said, 'Oh my god, look at this place! There's a million people's names on the ceiling,'" Ev said. "I put mine up there, of course, everybody did. I said to myself, 'Isn't this different? Isn't this nuts? This is crazy.'"

Sadly, Ev died just a few months after being interviewed for this book. A woman who did not care to dwell on mortality, Ev wanted no gravestone, no funeral, no obituary. There is little in the way of a memorial for this clever lady who so enjoyed her visits to the Mine Hill Tavern. But photographs of later renovations to the tavern indicate that portions of the much-autographed ceiling remains intact, under a layer of sheetrock. One has to wonder if the faded names of Ev—and many other departed Mine Hill Tavern habitues— remains intact, though hidden, under the ceiling of the main dining room of the property today, a poignant reminder that people who lived and loved had once passed this way.

"I remember one time—this is funny," begins Debi Alexander, who tended bar at Maddie's in the early 1990s, "I met my partner— we were together almost ten years—after I had started bartending. And I wrote 'I love Michelle' all over Maddie's in black permanent marker. Oh, Maddie was peeved, just peeved, because it wasn't chalk. But I was in such la-la land that I didn't care."

Though they had sold off their three gas stations prior to buying the Mine Hill Tavern, Frank and Maddie were apparently still short on the funds needed to start their new venture. So they approached their friend Hazel (Johnson) Lapadula, the proprietor of the nearby Torch tavern on Route 10 in Dover, for a loan.

"Hazel gave them some money for a down-payment on the place," said Harvey Klein, a longtime friend of Lapadula's who later tended bar at the Mine Hill Tavern. "I don't think Maddie ever paid her back, but Hazel was never charged for a drink when she came in."

Hazel was already a memorable local character when she started hanging around the Mine Hill Tavern. A robust woman of

---

[2] Ev and Marge asked that only their first names be used.

indeterminate sexuality and a red "rummy" nose from years of hard drinking, Hazel had a gruff exterior but a sensitive, giving heart. Klein described her as a Sophie Tucker type with a bawdy sense of humor and a way with a song.

"She was a very sweet and gentle woman," he said. "She had a gruffness in her voice that gave the appearance of, perhaps, toughness, but she was as gentle as a lamb. No matter where we went, they always had her singing with the band."

Her retinue was largely made up of parody songs, tunes like "Bye-Bye Blackbird" re-written with risqué lyrics.

Larry Winters[3] remembers Hazel vividly. In fact, she poured him his first beer, about fifty three years ago, when Larry was barely out of kindergarten.

"Do you know Route 10, where K-Mart is, in Dover? Right there, where you turn in, there was an old tavern called The Torch," Winters began. "Sweet old Hazel Lapadula and her husband ran it. Hazel went both ways, though we didn't know it till years later. Anyway, my granddaddy took me in there when I was seven years old. It had a dirt floor and a pool table and a jukebox. Hazel, she had a face like a bulldog. Tough. She was a sweet old gal, she and her sister Marion. They poured me my first beer."

Former Mine Hill Police Chief Richard Lansing started on the Mine Hill force in 1966 and he, too, remembered Hazel well. Part of Lansing's job when he was on duty was to make sure the taverns in town closed promptly at 2 a.m. The Bellinis, however, never seemed to be able to close the bar on time. Maddie, in particular, was annoyed by Lansing because of his constant enforcement of the 2 a.m. rule. Then one winter night Hazel slipped on the ice and injured her leg after a night of drinking at the tavern. She was lying out in the parking lot in a good deal of pain, but Maddie was reluctant to call the local police because she so disliked having to deal with Lansing. Instead she contacted the police department in nearby Randolph and they, in turn, alerted Lansing to the situation.

"I pulled up to the scene, and there's Hazel lying on her back, Maddie's bending over her," Lansing recounted. "I remember what Hazel did to this day. She looked up and said, 'Oh sh*t, Maddie.

---

[3] *Not his real name.*

155

That's the guy you don't like!' And Maddie said, 'Shut up you goddam fool! Shut up!'

"Then one night some time later, I was sitting in my car on the corner of Canfield Ave. and Route 46 at about 2:30 in the morning. There was a Mobil station there. I was just watching traffic. Right across from that intersection there was an embankment. Now there's a shopping center there, but it wasn't there at the time. Maddie come out of Canfield Avenue, never stopped at the light, went right across the highway and up the embankment.

"I go over there and open the car. There's Hazel, she's in the back seat, drunk. Maddie is drunk. And all Hazel can say is, 'Oh sh*t Maddie, it's *him* again!'"

Still laughing, Lansing adds, "The three people that were most closely connected to the Mine Hill Tavern, in my mind, were three women: Madeline Bellini, Hazel Lapadula and Maureen Kavanaugh."

Maureen Kavanaugh was the first barmaid the Bellinis hired, a decision that would have a profound impact on the couple's marriage and on the future of the tavern.

As part of a videotaped interview conducted by tavern regular Stephen Burns[4], done just before she sold the bar in the mid-1990s, Maddie was asked, on-camera, whom was the first she hired at the bar. Maddie responds, "Maureen." She's then asked if she and Frank had run the bar by themselves previous to hiring Maureen. "Right," Maddie says. "I did most because Frank got sick, ya know? Maureen was the original."

By 1964, Frank Bellini's almost constant partying was catching up to him. Described by friends as a handsome man who physically resembled Dean Martin but who was more like Perry Como in his mild temperament, Bellini began suffering from alcohol-related ailments in the 1960s.

"My Uncle Frank had a serious drinking problem. He would take a big water glass full of VO [Canadian blended whiskey] and drink it down," said Carl Gladish, a nephew of the Bellinis and later a bartender at the tavern. "I'm not a rye drinker, but he could take a water glass and drink the whole thing right down. He was in St. Francis Health Resort once for his drinking problem for a little while,

---

[4] *Not his real name*

but he used to say the pain was so great that the only thing he could do was drink to kill the pain."

With Frank's health becoming increasingly unpredictable, the couple needed help around the bar. They advertised a position in the local paper and Maureen Kavanaugh got the job. Ironically, considering all that would later ensue, it was Frank who actually hired Kavanaugh. In her early twenties at the time, Maureen had something of a reputation locally as a freewheeling sexual adventurer.

"There are a lot of stories about Maureen," said Lewis Rothbart, a longtime friend of Maddie who later became a bar owner himself. "Maureen—allegedly—was a very, very beautiful, beautiful girl. She allegedly seduced the wife of the guy who owned [another bar] on Route 46 in Dover. He caught the two of them in bed. That's what broke up that marriage. Maureen was notorious. I don't know how she and Maddie got together."

Surprisingly, given her time and place, Kavanaugh seemed to be quite sexually liberated. One local woman, now a senior citizen and a longtime Mine Hill resident, remembers that Kavanaugh carried on flirtations with both she and her husband.

"Maureen Kavanaugh used to go to my brother's tavern, which he bought when he won the Irish Sweepstakes in 1953," this woman said. "It was a shot-and-a beer place. But Maureen and three or four sisters lived next door. They would come in every single night. Maureen would come in the afternoon, too, and shoot pool. Always, I'd come with my husband in the evening. He'd drink a beer and we'd dance to the jukebox. Maureen would hit on me and I'd say no thanks. Then I'd go into the ladies' room and she'd hit on my husband! So I'd wonder, 'Are you gay or are you bisexual?' It was only when I'd go to the ladies' room when she'd ask my husband to dance."

On another occasion, this woman said, her brother saw Maureen passionately kissing another local girl in his bar: "He said, 'Hey, listen, we don't allow that stuff in this place. If you're going to do that, get out.' Of course, he was a neighbor, so he couldn't throw them out completely. But then she ended up with Maddie."

A relationship developed between the two women, and Frank was soon edged off to the side. He rented a place on Glen Avenue in Mine Hill while Maddie and Maureen shared a living space upstairs from the tavern, in some of the same rooms that had been home to the property's owners dating back to James Cox and John Bone.

"I was in the service when they bought the place, and a few years after that, my Uncle Frank and her split up," Gladish said. "He was in a house down the road, renting an apartment and she was there with Maureen."

Not surprisingly, and through very little conscious encouragement on Maddie and Maureen's part, the Mine Hill Tavern began attracting a gay following. As soon as lesbians in the area realized that the tavern was owned and operated by female couple, they began dropping in to check the place out, according to some of the women who visited the bar during the 1960s.

There's a long-standing general assumption that the bar didn't start catering to a gay crowd until after Frank's death in the late 1960s, but Gladish, for one, doesn't believe that to be the case: "I think it started to happen before that, after he and my aunt separated."

"In the 1960s the Mine Hill Tavern was kind of an undercover gay bar," said Mickey Suiter, who in 1972 would help found the Gay Activists Alliance in Morris County (GAAMC), the state's oldest and largest gay/lesbian/bisexual/transgender organization. "There were people who knew about it, but I think it was more women than men."

Two of those women were Maggie O'Hara and her now-deceased girlfriend Barbara, who first began frequenting what was then known as Frank & Maddie's Mine Hill Tavern in 1967 or '68, shortly after the birth of Barbara's son Patrick. [5]

Patrick became a kind of Frank & Maddie's mascot from his toddler days until about age ten. Another lesbian couple, Celeste Fontaine and Louise Warner[6] sometimes joined Maggie and Barbara.

In the winter of 2003, Maggie, Celeste and Louise got together at Maggie's home in Succasunna for a group interview for this book.

"We first went there thirty five years ago, and in those days, it wasn't strictly gay," Celeste said. "There was a lot of mixture. I think

---

[5] *None of these are their real names. In several quotations to follow, the name Patrick is substituted for the individual's actual name. All other details are accurate*
[6] *Also not their real names*

over the course of the evening it would change, and more gay people would come in as the night wore on."

Of course, even in later years, when it was almost exclusively a gay bar, heterosexual folk were always welcome at Maddie's. As late as the 1990s, there were a few straights that were comfortable enough with the atmosphere at the bar that they became semi-regulars.

"I had a lot of fun working at my aunt's place," Gladish recounted. "A lot of straight people came in there, too. You'd be surprised. What used to get me was that a lot of straight girls used to go in there with gay guys. I made out pretty good with them a lot of times, because the rest of the guys in the place were gay. When I first started working there, the drinking age was 18. There were a couple of the gay girls, man, I'll tell you, they were good looking. I tried my best with them, but I never made it."

Emphasized Maggie O'Hara of the Frank & Maddie's era: "There was a wonderful mixture of straight and gay people, wonderful Mine Hill people, Randolph people, people from Mount Fern. Ernie Pickle was one of the holdovers from the old days."

Few of the "old time" local crowd realized that any change was occurring in the tavern's clientele or atmosphere, however. The gays tended to keep a lower profile when the miners, hunters and employees of Hercules and Picatinny were in the bar. But a slow transition was nonetheless taking place. Part of that was due to economic necessity.

On February 26, 1966, the Allen Wood Steel Company's Scrub Oaks Mine, the last working iron mine in the state, shut down operations for good. It marked the end of a multi-million dollar industry that had played a major role in the development of Mine Hill, and indeed, all of Northern New Jersey. 245 Allen Wood employees —almost all of them residents of the Mine Hill area—were now suddenly out of work. For nearly 100 years the Mine Hill Tavern had been known as a miner's bar. If it was to remain in business in coming decades, it could no longer depend on the iron industry to stay afloat.

At the same time, and quite by accident, Maddie Bellini began to find the audience that would turn her from a semi-popular local entity into what her friend Lewis Rothbart referred to as "an icon in the gay community, almost a legend."

Though Maddie and Maureen both would have balked if anyone dared refer to them as radicals or activists (actually, Maureen probably would have tossed anyone who made that kind of statement out of the bar), the establishment of a gay bar in Mine Hill was indeed a revolutionary idea. With a population of about 3,500, Mine Hill was still a tiny rural community in the 1960s, peppered with farms and heavily forested. Indeed, even today the population is not significantly higher than it was in the late 1960s, and there are wooded areas of the township that still support a significant population of wildlife and where orange-capped hunters are commonplace.

Although there was an influx of New York transplants to the area in the 1990s, Mine Hill remains largely a working class haven in the early twenty-first century. It was much more so in the mid-1960s, a time when the only other gay bars in the state were in urban markets like Newark, Atlantic City, Trenton and New Brunswick. That's not surprising, of course. Gay communities traditionally spring up in metropolitan areas, where members of that community can cluster in the relative safety of anonymity.

But even in urban centers like Manhattan, gay bars could be enormously dangerous places to gather in the 1960s. There was constant threat of police raids, for example, the result of which was often public disclosure of the bars' customers, which at the time could mean the loss of a job and a home and the disintegration of one's family.

In New Jersey the very existence of gay bars was legally questionable until November 6, 1967, when the state supreme court ruled that gays had the right to gather in bars "so long as their public behavior conforms with currently acceptable standards of decency and morality."

The case came before the court when the state Division of Alcoholic Beverages (DAB) suspended or revoked the licenses of three gay hangouts—One Eleven in New Brunswick, Val's in Atlantic City and Murphy's Tavern in Newark—and the tavern owners challenged the decisions. The *New York Times* reported that the major question of the supreme court ruling involved the specific community "standards" and whether the customers at the three bars had violated them. In the mind of the investigator for the DAB, the following behavior by the tavern patrons was apparently enough to merit a suspension or revocation of liquor licenses:

"They [the homosexuals he encountered at the three bars] were conversing and some of them in a lisping tone of voice, and during certain parts of their conversations they used limp wrist movements to each other," the investigator testified. "One man would stick his tongue out at another and they would laugh and they would giggle. They were very, very chummy and close. When they drank their drinks, they extended their pinkies in a very dainty manner. They took short sips from their straws; took them quite a long time to finish their drinks. They were very, very endearing to one another, very delicate to each other."

The court ruled that this behavior was insufficient to warrant future action by the state, and the bars were allowed to reopen as gay clubs. So, at the very least, Maddie and Maureen would have had reason to believe their little tavern could not be shut down merely because it was a gay bar, if they even knew of the supreme court decision.

As the transition from blue-collar straight tavern to a gay one slowly took place, Frank & Maddie's regulars were sometimes witness to humorous or unusual scenes. Maggie O'Hara, for example, recounted a tale from this period, when her lover's little boy, Patrick (whom she helped raise and considers her own son), made a famous trip to the Mine Hill Tavern rest room.

"Ernie Pickle was an old railroad man," O'Hara began. "My son, Patrick was just a little guy. In those days Barbara and I used to bring Patrick with us to the bar. So one night Patrick went in the men's room and Ernie Pickle went in after him. Patrick's trying to go to the bathroom in the urinal, but of course the urinal was too high for him. So Ernie says to him, 'Patrick, you can't go to the bathroom in there. You're too young. You gotta pee in the bowl.' So Patrick's going to the bathroom and Ernie Pickle's going to the bathroom in the urinal and Patrick looked up at Ernie and said, 'You got a little one too, huh Ern?'"

Finished relieving themselves, the two fellows headed back into the bar, but Pickle was obviously disturbed by Patrick's comment. Maddie noticed Ernie's distress right away, O'Hara said, and asked him what was wrong.

"You ain't gonna believe what that little kid said to me," Ernie replied, recounting the incident for Bellini. Roaring with laughter, Maddie ran over to tell Maureen the story, and before Ernie realized it, Patrick's little observation had made its way throughout the bar and within a few days became a topic of local gossip.

There was, of course, one last string that was tying Madeline Bellini to her past life as a conventional wife in a conventional marriage. Though he did little, apparently, to inhibit her new life with Maureen, Frank Bellini continued to live near his estranged wife, and had occasion to stop by the little tavern he purchased with Maddie from time to time. Indeed, the tavern's liquor license remained in Frank's name.

That was all about to change, however. In early June of 1969, former Mine Hill Police Chief Richard Lansing—who was then a Sergeant—received a phone call from another local officer.

"At five o'clock in the afternoon on June second, Sgt. Leopold called me at home and said, 'Frank Bellini is dead. Can you come up and give me a hand?,'" Lansing recounted. "He died in bed with a bottle of booze alongside of his bed. His girlfriend told us how they had made love and then they took a nap and Frank never woke up. He had made love with this woman before he died."

It's kind of nice to know that, like Maddie, Frank had a companion to share his life with, and at least he died happy, in a post-coitus snooze. But his alcoholism had had a profound effect on the condition of his body. Drink enough alcohol, and one runs the risk of jaundice, a disease of the liver that causes one's skin to turn waxy yellow.

"By the time the medical examiner got there Frank was as yellow as this," Lansing said, pointing to a picture of the yellow-hued Homer Simpson on the cover of *TV Guide*, "The doctor said, 'This is the worst case of yellow jaundice I've ever seen.'"

Days after Frank's death from cirrhosis of the liver, his liquor license was transferred to Maddie, but only conditionally, for a period of two weeks. Frank, it seems, had failed to keep up with his taxes, and had thus imperiled the license, leaving Maddie somewhat vulnerable. Documents found at the township clerk's office show that Frank had failed to pay municipal taxes from 1966 through 1969, and was carrying a tax debt in the amount of $1,869.36 (the equivalent of $9,159 today), including almost $900 in Personal Taxes (about $4,400 today).

"It is imperative that you pay at least the Personal Tax before June 30th in order to have your license renewed," Municipal Clerk Virginia Shea wrote to Maddie in a letter dated June 14.

On June 6, Shea issued a liquor license to Maddie, "granting privilege of operating alcoholic business until June 30, 1969 under authority of license C-3 issued to Frank Joseph Bellini, now deceased."

Maddie must have come up with the money to cover the unpaid taxes, because she would continue to operate the tavern on her own for the next quarter century, which would turn out to be some of the most unusual 25 years in the property's already colorful history.

Just three weeks after the liquor license was transferred into Maddie's name, on June 27, the police raided the Stonewall Inn, a gay bar in the Greenwich Village neighborhood of New York City, forty five miles and a world away from Mine Hill. The raid on Stonewall was not in itself an extraordinary event. In 1969 raids on gay bars were conducted regularly, and without much resistance. What made the Stonewall raid remarkable was the fact that, for the first time, gay folks resisted arrest. Hurling beer bottles at the cops and inciting violent protest, the crowds in the bar fought back. The five nights of protest that followed came to be known as the Stonewall Riots.

For the gay community, it was a moment tantamount to Rosa Parks refusing to sit at the back of the bus. It galvanized gays as a minority group and changed the perception of the gay community forever. Prior to that summer there was little public expression of the lives and experiences of gays and lesbians. The Stonewall Riots marked the beginning of the gay liberation movement, a movement whose impact is still being felt by ordinary citizens in communities large and small throughout the country.

Now growing numbers of gays and lesbians would choose to live their lives openly and could congregate in public without fear of disclosure. Things were changing in America, and one tiny country tavern in Mine Hill, NJ was changing right along with it.

Still, the 1960s was not the open era of today. Most of the gay and lesbian customers at Maddie's Mine Hill Tavern during the Stonewall era would have kept their sexual orientations to themselves when not in a safe environment like the one Maddie and Maureen provided. Few were willing to be stigmatized by society because of who they were.

"We were trying to live our lives," Celeste Fontaine said. "We didn't want stamps on us."

Ironically, though Madeline Bellini and Maureen Kavanaugh were paving new ground in the creation of a gay community in Morris County, neither would have wanted to admit it. Indeed, when asked in later years just how the Mine Hill Tavern had become a gay bar, Maddie always tried make it appear that it all had nothing to do with her. She had a series of stock answers, stories that may have had just enough truth to make them seem plausible, but were likely not much more than smoke and mirrors.

One story had it that a gay couple, driving through New Jersey on the way home to New York City after a weekend in the Poconos in the late 1960s, had gotten themselves lost in the back roads. Stopping for a drink at Maddie's, they were allegedly charmed by the rough-hewn grittiness of the place.

"My, wouldn't this make a great gay bar!," they were alleged to have said to Maddie, and then went on their way. Upon arriving home in Manhattan, the couple phoned Damron, a company that publishes restaurant and bar guides for gays, and recommended they include Maddie's Mine Hill Tavern on their list of New Jersey gay establishments. When the next Damron guide came out, voila! Maddie suddenly found herself flooded with gay customers!

The beauty of this story, of course, is that it takes Maddie's own sexual orientation, and her role in establishing a gay bar, completely out of the equation. And it has a certain credibility to it.

Damron did, in fact, list Maddie's Mine Hill Tavern in their directories for several years, and according to Damron employees contacted for this book, it's certainly possible that someone simply phoned up the company and recommended Maddie's for placement in their publications. But their policy is always to follow-up with a phone call to verify that the establishment in question is indeed a gay bar. So Maddie or Maureen would have had to have given them clearance to publish the name of the tavern in their guides.

Told this story recently, Larry Winters, who first set foot in Maddie's in 1972, scoffed. "It didn't just become a gay bar all of the sudden," he said. "It happened over a long time."

Another version of the "How Maddie's Became a Gay Bar Story" that Maddie liked to tell involved members of a local gay activist group and their after-meeting barhopping excursions. This tale was told to—among others—Morris County Sheriff Ed Rochford, who is one of Maddie's nephews.

"My wife and I used to stop by my Aunt's place every year around Christmas to say hello," Rochford said. "And every year we would walk in, sit down and there wouldn't be anyone there except a couple of people. Well, we went up one year, it was in the mid-1980s and I think it was a Monday or Tuesday night. I pulled into the parking lot and it was full. I thought, 'What is going on here?' So I opened the door and the place was mobbed—wall-to-wall people, standing and sitting. You couldn't even get in there.

"I worked my way to the bar and all of the sudden somebody sitting at the bar turns around and says, "Ed, I never thought I'd see *you* here!" It was somebody I had known for years and years. So I said, 'Hey! How are you doing?' And he said, 'What are you doing here?' I said, 'Well, my wife and I came in...' And he said, 'Oh. You're still married.' And I said, 'Yeah, I've always been married!' And he told me he was gay.

"My Aunt told me the Gay Activist Alliance of Morris County used to meet on a Monday or Tuesday night and apparently after the meeting they would go to a different bar each time. Well, they went to my Aunt's bar one night. It was kind of empty. They put the jukebox on and the girls started dancing with the girls and stuff like that. At the end of the night one of them asked my Aunt if she was okay with all that and she said, 'Why shouldn't I be? You're customers just like everybody else.' So word got out that the owner was friendly and she didn't care what went on and the place got mobbed. She did very well. All of the sudden business picked up tremendously and she had several offers to buy the place that she had to turn down. It turned into quite an interesting place."

It's true, as Rochford discovered, that GAAMC members often stopped by Maddie's after their meetings on Monday nights, but that was years after Maddie started catering to a gay crowd. Once again, Maddie had found an explanation that allowed her to distance herself from her own groundbreaking creation.

CHAPTER EIGHT

The birth of GAAMC, the death of Marion Green and the beginnings of a local phenomenon

Maddie's Mine Hill Tavern—as it was called from 1969 through 1994—was not a glamorous place. It was dark and dingy, with a plywood floor that began to rot almost as soon as Frank Bellini and his nephew Butch installed it over the bare ground. The bathrooms were not exactly hygienic. The barstools were wobbly, the glassware eclectic. There was little air circulation to speak of, and the bar filled up with cigarette smoke as soon as one or two patrons lit up.

"Maddie's was very, very smoky," said Stephen Burns, a Maddie's regular from 1978 through the mid-1990s. "After a half-hour in there your clothes smelled like a cigarette and had to go right into the wash."

"Maddie's really wasn't an elegant place," said the aforementioned Marge, who used to frequent the tavern with her longtime companion, Ev. "It was the pits!"

"It was a dump," said the aforementioned Larry Winters. "But it was *our* dump."

It wasn't just the spartan decor and the poor air circulation that gave Maddie's a reputation as a "dump," however. In 1974, the Randolph Township municipal offices sent Maddie a letter reminding her that "on at least three occasions the Randolph Township Department of Health has received water analysis from two different laboratories in the State of New Jersey indicating the water supplying your establishment is bacteriologically unsafe. It is hereby ordered by the Health Department that you connect to the city water within the minimum amount of time as required by the utility that controls public water, in the town of Mine Hill.

"Failure to abide by this notice will result in closure of your establishment per Chapter 12."

Further, the Health Department helpfully—if somewhat ungrammatically—advised Maddie that "if someone becomes ill they would have the opportunity of blaming your establishment for causing the illness because of the present problem, even though it may be very true that this person in question, did not get sick in your establishment it is our opinion from past experience, that you would be in a very precarious legal position if this did happen and they filed suit against your business."

In a sanitary inspection report from the same year, Maddie's Mine Hill Tavern was found "conditionally satisfactory," though the inspector found such conditions as dirty surfaces, dirty kitchenware and "equipment and plumbing not installed and maintained as required by law."

"Dump" or not, for a very long time, there was simply nowhere else to go to meet people if you were gay and lived in Morris County. Emphasized Marge, "Actually the only reason we went there was because there were other gay people there."

A big part of the unique appeal of Maddie's Mine Hill Tavern was Maddie herself. A warm-hearted, outgoing presence, her customers were known to throw their arms around her and chat her up as soon as they entered the bar, before they ordered their first drink.

"Maddie would hang out with you. A lot of times she'd come around to the other side of the bar and have a couple of drinks," said Sheridan Willis, one of the few "straight" Maddie's regulars. "She and I were good friends and we'd talk about things. She always had such a great time. She made a lot of friends there. A lot of people enjoyed her. You could always go there and tell her your sorrows. I'd buy her drinks and she'd buy me drinks. That's why I don't remember a lot. I always did shots of Goldschlager. After you do two of those, forget it. Fortunately I didn't live far from there and my boyfriend didn't really drink."

"A tavern takes on the personality of the people that are running it," said Lewis Rothbart, who would open a gay bar of his own within a few years. "She was outgoing and liked to party and liked to do what she did. People responded to that. She was very pleasant, a good hostess. A really nice, kind person. She'd never hurt anybody. She liked to drink, and she could put it away. But she could hold it."

Asked if he thought Maddie enjoyed operating the little tavern, Rothbart said, "Oh yeah, there's no question about it. It showed. She loved the business, she loved the people associated with the business, she loved the customers, she liked being there. She really liked being there."

If Maddie was almost universally adored by her clientele—and no one interviewed for this book had less than admiring things to say about her—her companion Maureen was less so. While Kavanaugh had many friends among the Maddie's crowd, there were at least an equal number of people who disliked her.

After becoming a Maddie's regular in the late 1970s, Burns stayed away for a while because Kavanaugh was consistently uncivil to him. Late in the 1980s he again became a frequent presence at the bar.

"I never had any respect for her," Burns said of Maureen. "Most people had a kind of attitude of, 'Well, she's Maddie's friend, so let's be nice to her.' But I didn't see any point to that because I didn't like the way she acted. She drank Fleishman's, a brand of whiskey that was never in the bar, because as soon as Maddie would buy it, Maureen would drink it as fast as it appeared.

"She was a real professional drunk," Burns added. "Maddie didn't mind drinking, either, but Maureen was a nasty drunk. Sometimes Maddie would have Maureen behind the bar, bartending and drinking happily ever after, and she would be very very nasty to all kinds of different people, mostly guys. She was very jealous because Maddie always got along with everybody. Maureen didn't always get along with everybody. Maureen particularly didn't like me, as well as another person who was often in the bar. That person and I used to laugh about who she hated the most, me or him."

Kavanaugh was unable and unwilling to control her drinking, and the people around her were unequipped to deal with her alcoholism. That she had a constant supply of free booze added substantially to the problem. On literally thousands of occasions she became too intoxicated to climb the stairs to the living quarters she shared with Maddie. Sometimes she would simply pass out at the bar, or on the pool table. On occasions such as this a bartender or one of the customers would carry Maureen upstairs. Because she could be so loud and antagonistic when intoxicated, there were bartenders who—by their own admission—would purposely feed her more booze so she would pass out and they could take her upstairs and get her out of the way.

Often, Maureen would awaken from her alcohol-induced slumber after a couple of hours and realize that the bar was still open downstairs. More often than not she would find herself locked in, but desperate to rejoin the party, she would climb out her window and attempt to shimmy down the exterior railing on the front of the tavern. Usually she would fall, with a loud thud, to the ground below. She rarely injured herself, however.

"Whew, could she drink," said Carl "Butch" Gladish, a nephew of Maddie's who also tended bar. "I used to have to carry her upstairs, but she was light. She didn't weigh anything...She'd fall over the banister and onto the blacktop, yeah. She didn't hurt herself, either. Most of the time she didn't, anyway. Another time she had to get stitches in her head. They had the rescue squad up there. She used to fall off of the bar stools and hit her head all of the time, too."

Bartender Chuck O'Neill said that "Maureen's whole life was up the stairs and down the stairs. And Patsy Cline. And every morning at 4 a.m. she'd watch *I Love Lucy*...And then there were people who used to come in and get her going. As much as some people said they disliked her, they would come in and buy her drinks and get her riled up. They wanted to see her act up and throw ashtrays."

Harvey Klein, who started tending bar at Maddie's in 1971, said he mostly got along with Maureen, though he acknowledged that she could be difficult when intoxicated.

"Basically she was a very nice girl. She was a hard worker, she'd never miss a day. That was her only problem, that she could be a pain if had too much to drink. But that happens to everybody."

Maggie O'Hara liked to come into the bar in the afternoons during occasional periods of unemployment. She'd sidle up to the bar and watch game shows on TV while the little boy she was raising with her longtime companion played pool with Kavanaugh. O'Hara said that Kavanaugh doted on the little fellow like a beloved aunt.

"My son, my little guy, would come in with me," O'Hara said. "I came in one afternoon. I was out of work at the time. I started to watch *Jeopardy*. I put Patrick on the stool to shoot pool with Maureen. He was the only child allowed to shoot pool at Maddie's. They would put chairs around the pool table for him and he would shoot pool and he'd never scuff the green. He got through one day and this woman came in with her son, and they both started to shoot pool. Maureen said, 'No children on the pool table.' This woman said, 'That other little kid was allowed to shoot pool.' Maureen leaned over the bar and said, 'That's no little kid. That's Patrick. And Patrick shoots pool. Your kid doesn't.'

"Maureen loved Patrick, but there were people who would come in and deliberately try to get Maureen going."

Added Celeste Fontaine, a longtime friend of O'Hara's who was also a Maddie's regular: "Maureen wasn't always the easiest person to like, but some people would antagonize her."

As the bar's popularity grew, Maddie brought on a small roster of bartenders to work at the tavern. Among them was Klein, an enormously personable fellow who had been a successful professional dancer prior to working at Maddie's. As "Edward Kirk," his stage name, Klein danced on TV's *Arthur Murray Dance Studio*, in films like *Meet Me In Las Vegas* and Broadway shows like Ethel Merman's *Gypsy* and in a solo act he put together for nightclubs like the Latin Quarter or Copacabana. Occasionally, in fact, a customer would recognize him and say something like, "Didn't I see you on *Arthur Murray* a few years ago?"

"It was one of the most fun, nice places," Klein said of Maddie's. "You met all kinds of people there. Maddie was such a good-hearted woman. When the holidays came, she'd put out a big turkey dinner for everyone. She was very, very good-hearted, and everybody really loved her. You couldn't help but love her."

Also occasionally working the bar during this period was a petit, fashionable blonde named Kitty Stenkowitz. Kitty was described as "a real lady" by bar patrons. Photographs from the late sixties and early seventies show a sleek-figured Kitty, in go-go boots and miniskirt, sitting demurely on a barstool between Maddie and Maureen. Stenkowitz was extremely feminine, with a taste for the soft and frilly. This was demonstrated by a story Klein told of waking up in an apartment Kitty once rented from Maddie above the tavern.

One night in the early seventies, Klein went out for a late dinner after work and left his car in the Maddie's parking lot. Returning to retrieve his car in the wee small hours of the morning, he asked Kitty if she could put him up for the night.

"When I woke up I said, 'Jesus Christ have I died and gone to heaven?' There were all of these pink satin sheets. She slept in pink satin."

O'Hara described Stenkowitz as "lovely and attractive" but not always lucky in love. Indeed, at one point Stenkowitz was sitting at the bar having a drink with her boyfriend of the time when the man violently shoved her from her barstool. Kavanaugh and O'Hara leapt to Stenkowitz's defense, grabbing the man and tossing him outside.

"We were young then and we were in good shape," O'Hara said. "I told the guy, 'You gotta go, Buddy' and I handed him off to Maureen and she dragged him out of there. Then I went to get Kitty and make sure she was okay. Her wig had come off when the guy knocked her down, and my son went and picked it up. He said, 'Here's your hair, Kitty.' And she said, 'Thank you, darling.'"

Klein said that he believes Kitty, today, is about eighty and a Pennsylvania resident.

The colorful and bawdy Hazel Lapadula also occasionally helped out at the tavern, according to Klein. Her sister Marion (Johnson) Green was a regular presence behind the bar beginning in the late 1960s as well.

Klein described Green as "a very, very tiny person. Very quiet and shy. Just the opposite of Hazel." Green resembled Maddie enough so that customers often mistook them for sisters.

In a videotape shot by tavern regular Stephen Burns, Maddie is asked about her early employees. After running through various names, an off-camera voice reminds her about Marion, whom she had not previously mentioned. "Marion?," Burns asks. "Who was Marion?"

"She was Hazel's sister," Maddie responds. "Then she was killed up here. It was hit-and-run. They never found out yet who did it. She was going to her boyfriend's with a six pack...Must have been twenty years ago."

The death of Marion Green became part of the lore surrounding Maddie's, but with the passage of time some of the facts surrounding the incident have become blurred in people's minds. Today several former Maddie's customers and employees can recount the story in much the same way Maddie did on Stephen Burns' videotape, probably because they heard that version directly from her.

They inevitably end the tale with, "and they never found out who killed her."

"It was a very, very foggy night. I remember I couldn't see two feet in front of me," said former Mine Hill Police Chief Richard Lansing of July 22, 1973, the night Marion was killed. "She was walking on West Randolph Ave. from the tavern and she got hit. I was at dinner and the Dover Police called me and said, 'They've got a fatal in Mine Hill. They're looking for you.' I said okay. I went up."

53-year-old Green lived at 391 South Salem Street in Dover at the time. According to tavern regulars, her boyfriend lived just behind Maddie's, on West Randolph. Lansing—as well as another individual who knew Marion—believes she may have been a bit intoxicated at the time, and it's also speculated that she also may have been walking in the road itself, rather than safely on the road's shoulder.

"Yeah, from what I remember, she was drunk," Lansing said.

The *Daily Record* reported that witnesses saw a car strike Marion at 10:50 p.m. near 153 West Randolph Ave., which is perhaps four houses from the tavern. It would have taken Marion a minute or two to walk that distance from her place of employment, so the whole thing happened very suddenly indeed.

The newspaper reported that Mrs. Mildred Ransom, 56, of Apartment 5 of the Dover Garden Motel in Victory Gardens, was charged with causing death by auto and leaving the scene of an accident. Police issued an all-points bulletin with information from the car she was driving. Ransom was apprehended at 2:45 a.m, just three hours after the incident.

"The woman who hit her was staying at a hotel in Victory Gardens," Lansing recalls. Her car was located in the parking lot of the motel by a Randolph Township patrolman. Asked why Ransom hadn't stopped her car after striking Green, Lansing said, "I don't remember. I'm not sure if she said she hadn't seen her. It was a very foggy night."

Marion's death shocked both her family and her friends at Maddie's, some of whom learned about the incident the following day from the front-page story in the *Record.*

"That was horrible, really," Klein said. "She was very close to Hazel."

About a year before Marion's untimely death, and inspired by the wave of gay activism that resulted from the Stonewall Riots in 1969, four young people—all between the ages of 18 and 21—held the first meeting of their new organization, Gay Activist Alliance in Morris County (GAAMC). Mickey Suiter was one of those four founding members.

"I was nineteen, maybe, when I came out," Suiter said. "That was in 1970. I had graduated high school right around the time of the Stonewall riots. In fact, the day after I graduated I took a bus into New York City because I wanted to find other gay people. I'd heard they were in 'the Village.' It was the middle of the day on a weekday and I couldn't find anyone. I said to myself, 'There are no gay people here.' And I went home. I remember reading about the raid at Stonewall a couple of days later."

Like Suiter, another early GAAMC member, Curtis Watkins, found himself traveling into New York City to try to meet other gay men in the early 1970s.

"I came out in 1973, when I was twenty-something," Watkins said. "Coming from a relatively middle-class family, I had been in the closet and for a long time didn't even realize I was in the closet. I was very naive. I had a friend who came out to me, and that's when it snapped in my head and I knew that's the way I had to go. We set out together like Hansel and Gretel in the forest. The first bar we went to was Charlie's in New York. That's how it all started out. We were just enlightened enough—products of the first wave of the baby boom—to say, 'This is what we have to do.'"

According to a history of GAAMC published in the organization's newsletter and written by David Morris, the current GAAMC president, "During the 1970s and early 1980s, GAAMC was at the forefront of many political activities (often led by the founder Mickey Suiter)."

Suiter frequently stopped in at Maddie's at the time, to play pinball and socialize with the crowd there.

"In the seventies I remember going to the Mine Hill Tavern," Suiter said. "A friend of mine from work would go there with some straight married women from work. They had a ball up there, as 'tourists.' I always liked the Mine Hill Tavern because it was small and cozy and they had a great pinball machine. I loved pinball at that time. I'd just go up and have a few beers and play pinball and meet people that way.

"And they had a very odd jukebox, with everything from Patsy Cline to disco."

Indeed, along with the chalk signatures on the ceiling, the jukebox at Maddie's Mine Hill Tavern—with as diverse a collection of 20th Century pop music as one was ever likely to find—was one of the most memorable aspects of the property. Over the course of a single night, the music of Otis Redding, Nat "King" Cole, Juice Newton, Bobby Darin, The Weather Girls, k.d. lang, Frank Sinatra, Brenda Lee, Tom Petty, Bette Midler, Ann Murray, Marvin Gaye, Connie Francis, Madonna, Hank Williams or Roy Orbison might be played consecutively.

But it was the Patsy Cline songs that people remember most vividly. There were at least a half-dozen Patsy Cline tunes on that jukebox, with *Sweet Dreams* and *Crazy* among Maddie and Maureen's favorites. When the first few notes of *Crazy* would waft out of the jukebox's speakers, Maureen would often announce, "I like that song, because that's me. I'm crazy."

"Maureen said she met Patsy Cline once," Klein said. "I have an album that Maureen gave me that Patsy Cline autographed for her. Oh my god that's way back. I think, if I remember correctly, Maureen told me that Patsy was performing in Roxbury or somewhere in this area. I think it was Kitty Wells that was touring with her. That was Maureen's thing. And she could sing like Patsy Cline, too. She had a great voice. She had a figure that wouldn't quit."

Another Maureen Kavanaugh jukebox favorite was George Strait's *Drinking Champagne*, not surprisingly a song about boozing and flirtation and regret.

I'm drinking champagne
Feeling no pain
Till early morning
Dining and dancing
With every pretty girl I can find
I'm having a fling
With a pretty young thing

175

> *Till Early morning*
> *Knowing tomorrow I'll wake up*
> *With you on my mind*

Tom Casey and Kevin Roos are a longtime couple who visited Maddie's every Friday or Saturday night for close to ten years. Casey said that while Maureen didn't like a lot of people, she felt rather warmly toward the two of them.

"Maureen was very fond of Kevin," Tom said. "She liked me, too, because she knew I was with him. But she liked him. They used to sing 'Drinking Champagne' together. She always was amused by him."

Interestingly enough, by the late 1970s Maddie's Mine Hill Tavern was becoming a local phenomenon. Either because of the colorful crowd that gathered there, or Maddie Bellini's magnetic personality, or because of the increased gay visibility in the 1970s or (perhaps most likely of all) because it was simply the only game in town—the bar started to attract more customers than it could accommodate. Crowds flowed out onto the sidewalk in front of the tavern and into the intersection of Randolph and West Randolph Avenues. Police were forced to monitor the intersection to avoid traffic fatalities. The crowds were so thick that Chief Lansing started to wonder where all these people were coming from. They certainly couldn't all be from Mine Hill, after all.

"I started running plate numbers, just for the hell of it," Lansing said. "People were coming from as far away as Westfield, Plainfield, South Jersey near Trenton, down the shore and New York City. There were doctors and lawyers. I guess at that time gay people tried to keep their identity secret. It wasn't as out in the open as it is today. Word got out that that was a place they were accepted and could meet other people. It was the first gay bar around in our area."

"I remember being in the bar when it was packed," Suiter said. "The place got really popular after a while, to the point where it was overflowing out onto the street, and it's right there on the intersection. The police didn't like that and they used to hassle people and force them back into the bar. And Maureen would be working the bar and be drunk out of her mind. There would be about 75 men and six women in the place. And she'd just decide she wasn't going to serve the men anymore. And that was it. She was not going to serve the men! Only the six women! She'd be yelling and cursing. She could be mean and nasty at times."

Many times when the tavern was at it's most jam-packed Klein would be working behind the bar, mixing drinks and pouring beer as fast as he could and inevitably falling behind regardless. With limited parking in the lot across the street from Maddie's, cars would be parked up and down Randolph Ave., past the bar now known as Joann's, which was a half-mile from Maddie's.

"There were lines out the door," Klein said. "The drinks would be passed from one person to the next. You'd never believe it. Never. I remember one night when the police closed the place down because people couldn't get in the bar so they were drinking outside. When it went to court, it was thrown out because Maddie had an inn license, which permits you to drink anywhere on the property. You could drink outside. But the cars would be parked passed Joann's. Being behind the bar was like being a machine. It was non-stop. You'd have to see it to believe it."

Burns also remembers this period well.

"Between Maddie's and Joann's, there actually wasn't a parking space to be found Randolph Avenue," Burns said. "Maddie's customers' cars went all the way down to Joann's, and the cars from Joann's came halfway to Maddie's, so both sides of the street were mobbed."

Despite the long, frenzied nights waiting on crowds of customers, Maddie often found that she didn't want the party to stop at closing. Quite frequently she would get into her car after shutting down the bar and ride over to Dover to see if there was still a drink to be had at the taverns there. Local ordinances allowed for bars and taverns to remain open an hour later in Dover than in Mine Hill. Lewis Rothbart used to work in one of those Dover bars, and that's how he first got a chance to meet Maddie.

"My brother owned a tavern in Dover called the Mark Scott Pub and Maddie was a customer," Rothbart said. "Now, I knew nothing about the bar business. I was kind of managing the place for him. This had to be 1977, and Maddie came in and introduced herself.

I think she was with Maureen. She and my brother Kenny got along really well. She drank a couple of afternoons there.

"The first week we were there in Dover, they changed the hours so that on Friday and Saturday evening we were allowed to stay open till 3 o'clock. Maddie asked if she could bring down her crowd of people, because at 1:45 a.m. they had to close and her people still wanted to drink. So I said, fine, it's business. I had no idea what kind of crowd she had there.

"Well, at a quarter to two on the next Friday, fifty gays come into the place. We had only a handful of people in the place, so it didn't matter. For the next few years, every Friday and Saturday we got a mob from Maddie's. They would come religiously."

Realizing the gay market in Morris County could accommodate other bars, Rothbart decided to go into the gay tavern business himself, and before long he was Maddie's only competition, a fact that did nothing to alter the tenor of their relationship. Maddie and Lewis remained very close friends until the end of her life.

"We opened the Chalet as a gay bar in Hopatcong. I think it was December of 1978 that we opened the Chalet, but we still had a big crowd coming in from Maddie's, because of our long association with them," Rothbart said. "That first year I met Maddie, I was in her place maybe a half-dozen times. And when we opened the Chalet, she became a regular there. We saw a lot of Maddie. And for the last ten years she was open, I was in there almost every night."

In later years, Maddie would say that the Mine Hill Police were very good to her, and that she had little trouble with them. And indeed, that appears to be the case for the most part. But as the crowds at Maddie's Mine Hill Tavern ballooned in the late 1970s, the police were paying closer and closer attention to the property. Maddie's customers began to complain that the police were becoming increasingly aggressive toward them.

"Sometimes I wouldn't even get across the street to the parking lot and the cop car would be zooming down the street, getting ready to follow me," Casey said. "I'd look at the policeman and say, 'What the hell are you doing?' Or sometimes I'd turn around and go right back in the bar, because I was so annoyed.

"Usually the cops would follow someone out of the bar, and nine times out of ten it would be us, because we tended to leave early so we'd be the first people out of the lot. I was always the one driving because I'd limit myself to one drink. After they'd pull me over, I'd even say to them, 'You're following the wrong guy. I'm not the drinker in the crowd.' They'd have me walking the line, touching my nose, all that routine. It was annoying. So I complained to Maddie— many of us did—and I think she might have talked to the police and I think maybe that helped. But they were very aggressive."

As president of GAAMC and a frequent Maddie's customer, Suiter heard the same kinds of complaints, and he and the rest of his organization decided to try to do something about it.

"There was a problem for a while with the police, when they would just follow people as they left the bar, and pull them over as soon as they got a couple of hundred yards away and check them for drunk driving or just to harass them," Suiter said. "We here at the organization actually had a meeting with the Mine Hill Police Department and discussed some of the problems they were having up there."

Lansing acknowledges that a certain amount of police harassment was going on outside Maddie's: "We had an officer that was banging them like crazy with tickets, harassing them," he said. "He caused some problems. The chief at the time, Chief Magnusen, made us go down there to Morristown and talk to the gays in their meeting. We had to go to these sensitive talks with the gays. When we got there, right in front of us would be two guys hugging and kissing each other."

It was an eye-opening experience for the Mine Hill cops, who also realized that some of the Mine Hill citizens they were sworn to protect and serve were members of GAAMC.

"We found out that other people from Mine Hill were at the meeting, who were gay," Lansing said. "The chief was like, "Oh sh*t. Look who's here!"

After some initial friction, Suiter said, the whole thing ended well, with the gay activists and the Mine Hill police coming to a peaceful resolution to their problems.

"There was one officer especially who was super homophobic, and he was an issue," Suiter said. "But we actually got somewhere with him, and the police understood what was going on there and it was better after that."

Better with the police, maybe. But there was a shadow hanging over the gay community as the new decade of the eighties dawned. The shadow of AIDS.

CHAPTER NINE

Tigers, shootings, mailmen and AIDS

The thing to remember about Maddie's Mine Hill Tavern, more than one regular has said, is that you never knew what you were going to find when you walked through the front door. You could be sitting there having a drink when you suddenly realize the fellow behind the bar is a respected local judge. You turn to your left and see that the person sitting next to you has taken out his teeth and placed them on the bar in front of him. Look to your right and you notice that there's a guy a few seats over who had been on *Hollywood Squares* the night before. Then there's a sudden crash outside. You run to the door and find barmaid Maureen Kavanaugh splayed out on the sidewalk in front of the bar. Once again she had toppled from the second-story exterior railed walkway in a drunken stupor. From this vantage point you have a clear view of the parking lot. There, you just might see a van parked at the curb with a live tiger inside. And why on earth has the postman's truck been parked in the lot all this time?

At just that moment, Kavanaugh might rise unsteadily to her feet, brush some hair from her forehead and growl, "Get me a f**kin' drink!"

Just another night at Maddie's.

"You absolutely did not know what was going to happen at Maddie's," Harvey Klein said. "There were times when I would bring members of the Rock River Country Club up there. And I remember a very prominent judge once wound up tending bar. You never knew what you were going to find when you went there, but it was usually a good time. That's for sure."

Among the more interesting folks Klein remembers from Maddie's was Wayland Flowers of "Wayland & Madame" fame. Wayland and Madame was a campy ventriloquist act that was a staple of TV in the 1960s, 70s and 80s. Flowers and his puppet, which bore a striking resemblance to Phyllis Diller, were regulars on such programs as *Laugh-In*, *Hollywood Squares* and *Solid Gold* and appeared on dozens of variety and talk shows before landing their own daily syndicated TV series, *Madame's Place*, in 1982.

In 1983 Flowers published the life story of his inanimate wooden friend, "Madame: My Misbegotten Memoirs." Klein said Flowers stopped in at Maddie's a couple of times while en route to entertainment gigs at the big Poconos resorts.

"What was his name? He worked with a puppet named Madame," Klein said when asked about the unusual folks who came to Maddie's. "He was so good. Flowers. He was there on a couple of occasions."

Though relatively discreet about his private life, Flowers left little doubt that he was gay. He appeared regularly at gay clubs and was featured in the gay-themed 1976 film, "Norman…Is that You?"

The "Encyclopedia of Gay, Lesbian, Bisexual, Transgender & Queer Culture," praised Flowers for his ability to "express on prime-time television the attitudes and desires of many gay men in the early days of gay liberation—views that would otherwise have been regarded as pointedly offensive to mainstream audiences—without censure."

He died of AIDS in Hollywood in 1988, at the age of 48. His puppet, Madame, was buried with him.

Another colorful character was Wallis Lutz, who was assistant fire chief of Greystone Park Psychiatric Hospital Fire Department and a member of the Great American Circus until his death in 1992.

"One interesting person who came there was a guy who's name was Wally. He trained cats for the circus and I think he also worked at the fire department at Greystone Park," Klein said. "He had a hand-carved model of the circus that I think went to a museum when he died. He was tremendous. He also did stunt flying with his daughter. I used to tell him that all I ever wanted to do was ride an elephant and be close to a tiger. One day he came in and said, 'Well, your one wish is going to come true. You can be with a tiger.' He had a 600-pound Siberian tiger out in his truck. When the circus was in Somerville, he called me and said, 'Come on over and be with the elephant.' So I got my leg in the elephant's trunk and he carried me around."

Currently on display at the Space Farms Zoo and Museum in Sussex, along with over 500 animals of more than 100 different species—including several varieties of big cat—is a one-of-a-kind complete miniature circus that Lutz carved by hand. Space Farms founder Fred Space remembers Lutz well. He confirmed that Lutz helped raise the big cats at his zoo and was often allowed to take tiger cubs off-premises to show to his friends. Other circus enthusiasts remember Lutz's fascination with elephants, and don't doubt that he was friendly enough with the traveling Great American Circus personnel to have arranged an elephant ride for Klein.

"Anybody could walk in there, from any walk of life," said Molly Chapel, a regular Maddie's patron beginning in 1990. "Maddie was like a little Jewish grandmother who would welcome you with open arms. You had auto mechanics drinking next to the unemployed, drinking next to doctors or lawyers or nurses or people in the stock market. It was a place where you could be yourself. Nobody had any pretenses. It was all about just being who you are and having a good time."

Molly was present on more than one occasion when Kavanaugh stumbled from the second-floor walkway and landed with a thud on the ground below. By 1990 Kavanaugh's falls from the walkway were a fairly common occurrence, but these borderline slapstick incidents had started many years previous to that.

"God be good to her, Maureen was a tough gal," said Larry Winters. "If she liked you, she liked you. If she didn't, she didn't. That's the way it was. We had some crazy times with her. We were sitting at the bar one time and somebody walked in and said, 'Some poor gal is laying on the street, eatin' dirt.' We went out there and there was Maureen. She'd flipped over the porch up there and laid there in the dirt. So we picked her up and brought her back inside and she said, 'Give me a f**kin' drink!' Tough? Oh dear god, you wouldn't believe. And the music played and the liquor flowed."

Every couple of weeks or so, Winters would head over to Maddie's to help her clean up and make minor improvements to the place. On one such day, the mailman pulled up to the curb in front of the tavern to deliver the mail. He and Winters talked for a while and realized there was a mutual attraction.

"We ended up out in the outhouse out there," Winters said, referring to the old shed behind the tavern that had been used as an outhouse during the Sadie's era. "A couple of hours later I come back, and Maddie says, 'Something's wrong. The mail truck's been out there for a couple of hours.' So I told her about it, and she said, 'You

S.O.B.! You want us to get into trouble?! What are you doin' with the damn mailman!'"

Randall Sonner first visited Maddie's in the mid-1980s. An attractive blonde in his early thirties at the time, Sonner said that the mixed crowd at the bar was often peppered with older folks who were trying their best to hold themselves together.

"If you had your own hair and your own teeth when you went in there, you were ahead of the game," Sonner said. He wasn't kidding, either.

"There was one fellow there who would take his teeth out and put them on the bar, because they bothered him," said one Maddie's regular who asked to remain anonymous, "So he would talk to everybody and converse and everything with his teeth out of his mouth. There was another fellow who was dancing or horsing around one night and he lost his bridge. It wasn't a full set of dentures. He didn't even realize it was gone until he got home. He went up to Maddie's a day or two later and they had discovered it on the floor when they were sweeping up. So he rinsed them off and put them back in his mouth and they were perfectly fine again."

Another Maddie's customer was known for his dreadful toupee. The wig was so appallingly bad that this man was given a derisive nickname for it. So let's say this man's name was Harry Hairpiece (which is, clearly, not his real name, but a variation on his nickname).

One day Harry was playing pinball with another Maddie's regular when he bent over to place more change in the game. As he returned to the standing position, he didn't realize that his toupee had gotten caught on another man's belt buckle. It hung there for a moment like a trapper's pelt until the other man saw it there and said, "What the hell is that?" Standing at the pinball machine as bald as a cue ball, Harry was unaware that the entire bar crowd had witnessed the—excuse the pun—hair-raising event until he looked over at the other man, saw the wig and said, "Give me my hair!"

Harry was a constant presence at the bar through the 1980s, though he remains extremely closeted today. His friends remember him coming to Maddie's literally every night for almost a decade. He was there so often that when he didn't show up, his friends would worry that he had become ill or been in an accident. Extremely concerned that anyone in his family or local community should find out he is gay, Harry would sometimes drive long, circuitous routes to the tavern out of fear that someone might be following him.

Eventually Harry began an unfortunate intimate relationship with a much younger man. Close friends recall that Harry had never been so closely involved with another man before, and that Harry had made arrangements to provide living quarters for the young fellow. But Harry's new companion was a deeply flawed human being. Sometime after the two launched their romance, according to several friends in whom Harry confided, the young man was investigated for having sex with a minor and soon thereafter committed suicide.

Obviously Harry was greatly troubled by this series of events, as much because of the damaged lives caused by the molestation charges and suicide of his young friend as by the fear of greater public scrutiny of Harry's own personal life. His visits to Maddie's became less and less frequent, until he stopped coming to the bar altogether. When contacted at his place of business recently, Harry claimed he had never been to Maddie's Mine Hill Tavern and knew nothing about it, despite the fact that a half-dozen individuals interviewed for this book knew Harry well, frequently saw him at the bar, and could recount the story of his unfortunate romance with the younger man who later committed suicide.

It should be pointed out, however, that the molestation/suicide story could not be verified through sources outside of tavern regulars. Neither interviews with local law enforcement officials nor searches through area newspapers of the 1980s could provide any verification for the story. It is possible, therefore, that the tale is simply bar lore.

Needless to say, Harry Hairpiece was not the only closeted individual to walk through Maddie's front door. Indeed Maddie and Maureen themselves often acted in a contradictory fashion in regard to public disclosure of their sexual orientation. Despite all evidence to the contrary, both would occasionally deny that they were lesbians. Maureen, in particular, would chastise anyone who suggested she and Maddie were gay.

"Let me tell you something," she was known to insist while leaning over the bar and jabbing her finger in the air for effect, "I'm not gay. And neither is Maddie."

Chuck O'Neill, who began tending bar for Maddie in the 1980s, would occasionally joke about his employer, deliberately calling her a lesbian to tease a response out of her. Finally, O'Neill said, Maddie took him aside and scolded him, saying, "Stop saying I'm a lesbian!"

"She never would admit that she had a relationship with Maureen," O'Neill said. "It wasn't acceptable and she didn't talk about it. But they went on vacations together, and when you went upstairs, and you'd think Maureen would be in her bedroom, she wouldn't be in her bed. She was in Maddie's bed. Maureen's room had nothing in it. There was a little bed, no clothing, no closet. There was something on the wall, but it looked like a room that nobody was ever in. Every time I went upstairs Maureen was always sprawled out on Maddie's bed."

Maureen was also occasionally seen with another woman whom, Winters said, Maureen would take upstairs to her room for intimate encounters, much to Maddie's extreme displeasure.

"There was a gal up the street. We used to call her Sarge," Winters said. "She'd come down to the bar. One time she come down and Maureen had Sarge upstairs in her room and Maddie threw a fit. Yeah, she called the cops and everything."

Maddie, too, obviously found other women attractive. Ev and Marge were regulars at the tavern since the 1970s. Marge, an Italian American beauty in her youth who was still an attractive woman in her later years, said Maddie often used to flirt with her: "When we would go in, Maddie would be behind the bar and she'd look at me and say, 'Ah! That's my girl!,'" Marge said "And she'd say to Ev, 'If you ever get tired of Marge, let me know!'"

If Maddie and Maureen were coy about their sexual orientation, they remained enormously compassionate toward the gay men and women who were their main customers. Realizing that many of her customers were estranged from their families, for example, Maddie kept the tavern open on holidays and provided buffet dinners for gay folks who had nowhere else to go.

"It was a payback to the community" longtime friend Lewis Rothbart said. "To provide a safe space for people who didn't have a safe space. I think that's why she stayed open on holidays and had food out. These people kept her in business all year, and this was her way of saying thank-you."

Tragically, the gay community in New Jersey would need all of the compassion Maddie could mete out in coming years. In 1981 the New York Times published its first article about AIDS, headlined, "Rare Cancer Seen in 41 Homosexuals." That year only 422 cases of AIDS were diagnosed in the U.S., and 159 were dead from the disease. The following year 1,614 cases of AIDS were diagnosed in the U.S. and 619 were dead. It was the beginning of a plague that would eventually infect 40 million people worldwide, and counting.

"The first person I knew that died of AIDS I knew from the Mine Hill Tavern," said Mickey Suiter. "He occasionally worked as a bartender there. You'd hardly even heard about AIDS yet, and within a space of three weeks he had gotten sick and died. His name was Don. I don't remember his last name. I lost a lot of acquaintances during that period."

On December 26, 1983, Donald W. Voorhis died at Lenox Hill Hospital in New York City. Known locally as "Trixie," Donald had tended bar off and on at Maddie's for several years. He had lived in Wycoff before moving to New York in 1981, where he worked as a bookkeeper for St. John's Church. He was only 32 years old.

"He was very outgoing and humorous and a very sweet guy," said one of Don's old friends. "Not a bad word to say about anybody. Very friendly and outgoing. He attended a few parties at my place when we lived at Hopatcong borough, which is different from Lake Hopatcong, where I live now. My lover, who has since passed away, was a little friendlier with him than I was...He was busy into having a good time and was deep into gay life and everything like that. In those days we were carefree and thought about when the next party was going to be and that sort of thing."

Two and a half years after Voorhis died, another tavern regular, Succasunna resident Dean Allan Ross died at Dover General Hospital. Heart-breakingly, Dean was only 27 years old.

"What a beautiful young man," said Maggie O'Hara. "His parents came in one day and I knew he had AIDS and I went over and told his mother, 'I'm so sorry about Dean.' And she said, 'I know, thank you.' And I said, 'How is he doing?' And she said, 'He's in a coma.' His father couldn't deal with Dean's homosexuality, and I don't think it was too long after that that his mother and father separated for good. Everybody loved Dean."

"Dean was an exceptional artist," Stephen Burns wrote via email. "He moved to Florida for a while and was noted for creating incredible sand sculptures in front of the legendary Marlin Beach."

The earliest AIDS casualties known by the folks who frequented the Mine Hill Tavern were perhaps the most memorable, but there were many more to come, some remembered now chiefly by nickname—"Tall Bobby," "Blonde Michael"—and some who were only remembered, if at all, by the scrawl of chalk on the ceiling of the little tavern.

The AIDS crisis ushered in a new wave of activism in the 1980s, and gays in metropolitan areas like New York, San Francisco and Washington, D.C. took to the streets in protest of government inaction on AIDS issues. Groups like ACT-UP aggressively fought for increased funding and public awareness of the disease. The activism created an enormous awareness of the disease and its cost to the gay community, and forced many closeted gays to come forward in support of AIDS causes. But this new visibility had a cost as well. A street-level backlash ensued, and incidents of "gay-bashing" rose alarmingly during the period. Groups of thugs descended on gay enclaves like the Village and Chelsea and brutalized those they believed to be gay for no apparent reason.

In New Jersey, GAAMC was at the forefront of the new AIDS activism, and ranks of the group swelled in the 1980s, making it the largest gay and lesbian group of its kind in the state. Unfortunately, Morris County would experience its own share of violence against gays as well.

"I'll never forget the time when these kids threw something at the window, and as old as she was Maddie ran out of there and jumped on the back of their car," said bartender Chuck O'Neill. "And the kids stopped. They couldn't believe that she jumped on their car, but you didn't mess with her."

Occasionally during the 1980s straight kids—mostly teenagers —tried to make trouble at the Mine Hill tavern by driving by and throwing eggs and shouting epithets. Few, apparently, got away with it for very long.

"A bunch of straights come in one night, started a lot of crap," Winters related. "They were throwin' rocks and stuff. These two gals intervened, but the straights got in their car. Maddie jumped on the back of the damn car and they were going down the street with her. She was fearless."

Sonner remembers another incident, when Maddie's was charging a cover charge at the entrance to the tavern because she had hired a D.J. that night. The cover charge was minimal, probably $1 or $2, but it was apparently too much for a group of guys who came into the bar and brushed past Maureen at the entrance.

"They didn't pay the cover, and then they started mincing around, like, "Oh look at us, we're at a *gay* bar," Sonner said. "Mostly everybody ignored them, but somebody must have called the cops. Maureen went over to them and asked for their cover again, and they refused to pay, so she grabbed the first drink she could find and threw it in one of the guys' faces. And all the sudden the police showed up. The guy who Maureen threw the drink at still had ice cubes from the drink lodged behind his glasses when the cops asked what was wrong. They told the cops that Maureen had thrown the drink. The cops asked Maureen if she had done so, and she said, 'No, I did not.' Then the cop turned to the rest of the bar and said, 'Did anybody see her throw a drink in this man's face?' And everybody was like, 'I didn't see anything.' So the guys ended up just leaving."

The fights at the bar didn't always end so quietly, however. Though rare, bar brawls did occasionally take place at Maddie's.

"We had a big fight down there one time," said Chief Lansing. "I'm surprised the guy didn't get killed. He went in there and started bad-mouthing the gays and they beat the crap out of the guy. There was blood all over the place. This had to be in the late seventies or early eighties. But by and large they kept most of their business to themselves. If they fought, they didn't want to call the police. I left them alone and they left me alone. By and large we got along. I got along with Maureen Kavanaugh, too. And she could be tough."

Once, Lansing said, he was called down to Maddie's and he found that Maureen had pinned another young lady on her back on top of the pool table.

"One night I go down there. Maureen had a fight with another female. Maureen had this woman on the pool table with a cue stick right down her throat. I said, 'Maureen, let her go. Let her go.'...But, to tell the truth, there was more trouble at a place called Joann's, down the street. In fact, the owner there had to pay the police every Friday and Saturday night to sit outside. But by and large we didn't have much trouble at the Mine Hill Tavern."

Joann Canfield, who currently operates Joann's, the tavern a half-mile down Randolph Ave. from what is now Cornelius House, remembers Maddie well. The two were close friends, Joann said. When Joann ran out of supplies like straws or napkins, she said, she would go down to Maddie's and replenish her stock, with Maddie's blessing. The two enjoyed a warm platonic relationship, often rooming together during conventions for the licensed beverage industry in Atlantic City. An enormously personable Asian-American woman, Joann had obvious affection for Maddie, who would sometimes come down the street for a drink or a bite to eat.

"She was a very nice lady," Joann said. "She would come in and eat a main course like stir fry or chicken. She loved shrimp cocktail. She'd drive down here and have a glass of wine and a shrimp cocktail. She had a friend, Maureen, who lived with her. She came here once in a while, too. But she was very, very heavy drinker. Always drunk. She only drink Irish whiskey."

Despite the fact that only a half-mile separated their two taverns, there was no sense of competition between the two women. In fact, Joann said, they were like sisters.

"We'd go to licensed beverage association conventions in Atlantic City. She'd always be hostess of Morris County. She'd run the hospitality suite. Sometimes there'd be a licensed beverage meeting and I'd say I didn't want to go, but she'd say, 'Come on. Let's go. You'll learn something.' So I'd go places with her. I felt comfortable with her. She was like my sister. She was a different age from me. A very warm person.

"One time I was supposed to meet her in Atlantic City, and my reservation didn't work out. So I didn't have a room. I said, 'Maddie, I don't have a room. What am I gonna do?' She says, 'Come stay in the hospitality suite, but I don't think you're going to sleep, because people will be in and out all night long.' she says, 'You could sleep in the hot tub!' I had a lot of respect for her, and learned a lot from her. So much."

Maddie's and Joann's catered to their own distinct crowds, but there was a little crossover.

"We used to go stop at Joann's on the way home from Maddie's," Lew Rothbart said. "That was a fun bar, too. Different crowd. She had her crowd and Maddie had hers."

Joann herself seems such a natural behind the bar that one might think she was born there. That was not the case, however.

"Do you know how I ended up with this bar?," she said. "My husband was shot by his girlfriend."

The biggest trouble to have occurred at the property now known as Joann's Bar took place a few years before it was known by that name. In August 27, 1984, Patricia Cycoveck called the Mine Hill Police to report a shooting. Joann's husband, Richard Canfield (who was the owner of Zeke's Pub, the name by which Joann's Bar was then known) had taken a bullet in the abdomen. Lansing was the first officer on the scene.

"The Friday night before the shooting, I was told by a girl that there were guns in the place. I'll never forget this as long as I live. Friday night I talked to this barmaid in the parking lot. She told me that [Richard] Canfield gave her a gun for protection. He told her, 'Anybody give you any crap, shoot 'em.' I wrote a report on it. I came back to work Saturday night, checked the bar, and everything was quiet. But Canfield and his girlfriend weren't there. They were in New York at a swinging club. They were swingers, Canfield and this broad. Sunday night at 2 a.m. I went to check the place to make sure it was closed, and nobody was there. No vehicles around, nothing."

Canfield was a gun collector and—by Lansing's account—a somewhat volatile individual. Though still married to Joann, the two were separated. In August of 1984, Canfield was living with his mistress, Pat Cycoveck, in an apartment above Zeke's Pub.

"I'm at the Traveler's Diner in Dover at about 2:30 a.m. when I get a call saying there was a shooting at Zeke's," Lansing said. "I went up there, I called for help. I called Dover, Roxbury, everybody. I said I was told there were guns in the place and there was a woman involved, there was a weapon involved and the woman was crying for an ambulance.

"We got to the scene," he continued, "but I didn't go in until other patrols responded. I told the dispatcher to keep the girlfriend on the telephone, to keep talking to her. We worked our way into the kitchen very slowly, because I had a feeling this Canfield was a nut. We could see her bending over somebody on the floor. She's crying. We said, 'Back away.' She said, 'But he's dying!' We said, 'Back away.' I had told the other officers, 'If he's partially alive and can get to a gun, be careful. He may take somebody down. He's an ornery guy.'

"We got her away and called the proper authorities. Then we made an investigation. We went upstairs and—this was very odd—every window upstairs over the tavern had guns lined up alongside the window. It was like he was getting ready to hole up there."

The Morris *Daily Record* quoted Morris County Prosecutor Lee Trumbull as saying "There had been some drinking going on," and Canfield fired five shots in rapid succession into the ceiling. Fifteen minutes later the couple went downstairs to the bar where another shot was fired, "during a discussion," Trumbull said. Then Canfield handed the .44 caliber single-action revolver to Cycoveck by the barrel and the gun discharged, Trumbull said.

"Her story was that he was showing her how to load a gun," Lansing said. "She blew a hole right in his gut."

Trumbull told the newspaper that it had not been determined whether the two were arguing before the shooting.

Cycoveck claimed the shooting was accidental, and a later grand jury believed her story. She was cleared of aggravated assault charges by a Morris County Grand Jury in December, 1985.

Lansing isn't so sure the gun went off by accident, however.

"No. I don't believe it, but the grand jury found differently," Lansing said. "I think she was mad because when they were in the city he was messing around with other women and everything. I think they were fighting. They went into the city, to this swinger's club, and

I think he was [expletive]ing women out there. She got annoyed, and I think she was also p.o.'d because he was trying to [expletive] the barmaid.

"Some people cannot own a bar. He was like a kid in a candy store. He thought he could [expletive] anything that came in the bar. That's my opinion. I think they were fighting and either arguing over the gun or something and she got the best of him."

Cycoveck has since moved from the Mine Hill area, and attempts to discover her whereabouts were unsuccessful.

The shooting of Richard Canfield had eerie echoes of earlier killings that occurred during Mine Hill's iron mining heyday. Like the Moore and Reilly murders, for example, it involved domestic discord and heavy drinking. And it occurred in the middle of the Irishtown section of the village, just a few doors away from the last surviving intact miner's dwelling in town.

The name Canfield even harked back to the town's iron mining glory days, when the Moore, Smith and Reilly murders occurred. Frederick A. Canfield and his father, also named Frederick, operated the Dickerson Mine for several decades during the peak iron-mining period in Mine Hill. Though Frederick A. Canfield left no direct descendants, a genealogy of the Canfields found in the Morristown Public Library suggests that nearly every living American Canfield can trace their heritage back to three Canfield brothers, Matthew, Thomas and Nathaniel, who lived in Connecticut in the 1600s. It's entirely possible, therefore, that Richard Canfield was a distant relative of the famous Canfields for whom Canfield Avenue in Mine Hill was named.

Interestingly, the Mine Hill detective who investigated the shooting incident at Joann's was a cousin of Richard Canfield. Contacted for this book, former Detective Charles Canfield chose not to comment, other than to say, "Maddie was a good person and we always got along good with her."

Maddie and Maureen resided close enough to Joann's to have heard the gunshots and the police sirens. At the time of the shooting, they would have been getting ready for bed after having straightened up the bar downstairs. The shooting would have been the talk of Maddie's Mine Hill Tavern for weeks to come.

After Richard Canfield's death, the tavern was inherited by his son, Young, who operated the property for about two years. His mother, Joann, then took over, renaming it after herself.

"Funny thing is, people think I did it." Joann said, referring to people who have heard about the shooting but mistake her for the shootist. "People ask if it was me [who shot Canfield], and I say, 'If I did that, how you think I stay here?' You know what I mean? Even when I go to bar association meetings, some bar owners think that I did it. I used to get very upset about that, but now I don't care. Think whatever you want to think."

Interestingly the very next interview conducted for this book, after the Joann Canfield interview was concluded, was with someone who knew Madeline Bellini and Joann Canfield fairly well.

"Joann's is an interesting story, too," this person said with great authority. "Joann shot her husband and killed him."

Four years after the shooting at Joann's that was likely the source of much speculation and gossip among Maddie and her customers, the bar crowd experienced a sad loss. Hazel Lapadula, who had been a fixture at the place ever since she had first helped finance Frank and Maddie's purchase of the bar back in 1961, died at Morristown Memorial Hospital on Friday, November 4, 1988.

Harvey Klein, who cared for Hazel for many years, said the bawdy old gal had been in very good health right up until the end of her life.

"They found a little cancer in her bladder," Klein said. "She came through the operation beautifully, but they told me that between the anesthesia that was used and the long length of the operation, it might have a serious effect on her, because of her age. The day before she was going to come home, she had a massive stroke and that's what took her."

Lapadula kept her wicked sense of humor right through her final illness however, even when a doctor was examining her before her bladder surgery.

"This is a very funny story," Klein said with a chuckle. "It's a thing about her with the doctor. She had a nose that you might call a rummy nose. A person who drinks heavily sometimes has that ruddiness to their nose. Well, the doctor has her feet up in the stirrup

194

and he's examining her down there. So he says to her, 'Were you a heavy drinker?' And she says, 'Can you tell that from down there?' And he said, 'No, by your nose.' When she came out of the examining room and told me that, that struck me as so funny. 'That goddam guy telling me [that about] my nose!' That was truly funny."

Hazel had been 79 and a lifelong Dover resident. Klein currently resides in her former home.

CHAPTER TEN

The last days of Maureen Kavanaugh, and the Mine Hill Tavern goes respectable

What you see here,
What you do here,
When you leave here,
Let it stay here.

That was the message on a sign hanging behind the bar at Maddie's Mine Hill Tavern. The bar was decorated—if that's what you'd call it—with dozens of kitschy items: mugs with Maddie's name on it, little toys, postcards from old friends, and a couple of other signs with memorable phrases. One of these signs read, "My cow died, so I don't need your bull."

Another sign hung from a rafter just inside the front door of the tavern, so it was the first thing a person saw when they entered the place. It read, simply, "This is it, M.H.T." The M.H.T. initials stood for Mine Hill Tavern. Like the chalk marks on the ceiling and the jukebox, the M.H.T. sign was one of the trademarks of the place. And like several other items of Maddie's memorabilia, the M.H.T. sign survives today, in the home of a longtime Maddie's regular.

"There were all kinds of postcards and little thingies behind the bar," said Sheridan Willis, who used to visit Maddie's in the early 1990s. "Some of that stuff was up there on shelves behind the bar for probably thirty years. Do you know what else I remember? The glasses. I don't think there were two glasses in the whole place that matched. Even the shot glasses—she had about three shot glasses that matched and the rest were all different. You never knew what you were going to get. Some looked like toothbrush holders. That made me laugh more than anything. Everybody had a different kind of glass. Some are big, some were small. Sometimes you got a beer in a big glass, sometimes in a medium-sized glass."

Indeed, it's doubtful that Maddie and Maureen ever paid anything close to full price for any of the glassware in the bar. Glasses were picked up at garage sales, or purloined from formal catered affairs Maddie was invited to, or from other taverns she visited.

"If she was staying in a hotel, she'd steal the glasses to use in her bar," said Stephen Burns. "If she went to a wedding, she'd steal the glasses!

"I used to like an occasional brandy when I went into the bar, but she had no brandy snifters. So one time I went to a garage sale and found brandy snifters. They were, I think, six brandy snifters for a dollar. So I bought them for Maddie. She said, 'Oh, those are beautiful!' Do you know what? She took them upstairs and never used them! I asked her, 'Where are your brandy snifters?' And she said, 'Oh, they're too good to use in the bar. People will break them.' I said, 'Maddie, I only paid a dollar for them! If they break it doesn't matter!'"

Maddie's habit of picking up glassware wherever she could find it may have rubbed off on one of her barmaids. This young lady, who worked at the tavern in the late eighties and early nineties, was a figure of some controversy. Because certain unverifiable statements have been made about her, and because she could not be reached to comment on these statements, both her name and certain identifiable characteristics about her have been changed. For the purposes of this book, this barmaid will be known as Brenda Foley. In the references and quotations to follow, that name is substituted for the individual's actual name.

Foley seems to have been disliked by many Maddie's customers, some of whom were said to have been financially victimized by her. On more than one occasion, for example, it was said that Brenda passed bad checks. This may have led to her arrest and incarceration in Dover.

"She was very attractive, beautiful. But she became very unpopular very fast," said Celeste Fontaine. "She was one of those people that just used everybody. She was always in trouble for bad checks. There was a time when eight or ten of us went out to a bar called Stockman's. The table had been full of empty glasses, but when we got up to go, there was not a glass left on the table. Brenda took every one of them. I was so embarrassed."

There were some Maddie's patrons who suspected that Brenda was interested in a romantic attachment with Maddie, but couldn't get very far as long as Maureen Kavanaugh was in the picture. Not surprisingly, Maureen was said to dislike Brenda in the extreme.

"Maureen hated her," said Chuck O'Neill. "She had such passionate hatred for her. She hated Brenda more than anybody. She would freak out when Brenda came in. Brenda is probably about fifty now. She had some wild life, that woman."

Kavanaugh herself continued to live a wild life into the 1990s, but a lifetime of heavy smoking and drinking was taking a terrible toll on her health and appearance. Though only in her late forties or early fifties when the decade of the nineties began, most tavern customers assumed she was far older. One customer actually had the nerve to directly ask Maureen about her age. Maureen fixed him with a cold glare and said, "How old do you *think* I am?"

Making the mistake of answering her question honestly, the young man replied, "Umm, seventy?" She refused to serve him a drink for the rest of that night.

"You never wanted to be on Maureen's bad side, or you'd never walk back in there," said Molly Chapel. "She was just one of those people that, if you even looked at her the wrong way, she'd never serve you again. You could be the only person in there and still she would never serve you. She was always drunk herself. Towards those latter years she was really starting to be pretty ill. I actually remember more often than not being there and the ambulance would come and take her out to the hospital. That happened on a number of occasions. That was when Chuck O'Neill was bartending."

By all accounts Maddie was extremely fond of O'Neill, and she depended upon him greatly through the early 1990s. O'Neill was the only employee entrusted to a key to the tavern, for example, and he often was forced to help both Maddie and Maureen upstairs to their living quarters when the women had had too much to drink.

"I'll never forget, there was a Sunday afternoon when this handsome guy came in the bar," O'Neill said. "He had never been in the place before. Maureen was drunk and spinning around the room. She whacked her head on the pay phone and fell down, passed out. I slapped her on the face a few times, but she wouldn't move. So I

199

asked this guy who was in the bar if he would do me a favor and help me carry Maureen upstairs to bed.

"It was the summer. He had shorts on. We picked her up, and she was dead weight. The next thing you know, her bladder went, and she went all over us. The guy drops her and I started screaming, 'Maddie! Maddie! She's dead! She's dead!' When somebody dies, their bladder goes. So another guy came over and wrapped her in a towel and carried her upstairs. Maureen was a nightmare but also part of the charm of the place. She threw everybody out, she was out of control."

Recalled Molly Chapel: "There were times when she'd be sitting on a bar stool and she'd just pass out cold and the next thing you knew she was on the floor. I did feel bad for her, but of course it was also comical. She knew it was comical. She'd laugh about it and then do it again the next night."

She may have tried to maintain a lighthearted exterior, but Maureen was increasingly in pain and discomfort. She continued to tend bar through the first half of 1992, but there were more and more trips to the hospital as the year went on.

"Maureen got really sick the last couple of years before she died," O'Neill said. "I think she had throat cancer. She was in the hospital for months and months. They finally brought her back home in an ambulance. They took her up those rickety outdoor stairs to her room on an ambulance gurney. They put her to bed, but after they left, she snuck downstairs.

"She wasn't supposed to have any alcohol, and I wouldn't give her a drink. She couldn't even speak, but she was going for a bottle. I told her 'No-no-no,' but as soon as I turned my back she took a shot. No sooner had she done that that she was back in the ambulance and back at the hospital. She started going into convulsions or something after that first drink. I don't think she was even home for ten minutes."

Larry Winters believes the source of Maureen's anger was jealousy over the attention that many customers showered on Maddie. These same customers tended to ignore Maureen except to order a drink.

"All Maureen wanted was recognition," he said. "When you're in the public eye the way Maddie was at the bar, all of these gals would come in and they'd play on Maddie's affections. They knew that that bothered Maureen, so they bugged the hell out of her. She just couldn't handle it, the poor woman. She was stuck there. She couldn't drive, she was an alcoholic.

"One of her last wishes was to go down to the sea shore. She asked me if I would take her. But she had this tracheotomy thing in her throat and I wasn't sure I could handle it if something happened. So I made some excuse that I couldn't take her. I feel so bad about that. I should have taken her."

While working at a popular restaurant in the area, Maggie O'Hara and her adopted son Patrick also encountered Maureen near the end of her life.

"My son adored Maddie and Maureen," O'Hara said. "When he was a grown man, years after we stopped taking him to Maddie's, I was tending bar at a restaurant and Maureen was very sick, near the end of her life. Maddie and Maureen both came in while Patrick was at the bar. I said, 'Patrick, Maureen and Maddie are over there.' I didn't tell him to go over and say hello, because I think too many mothers do that. But he went over there on his own.

"He turned to Maureen and said, 'You don't say hi to an old pool buddy, huh?' She looked over at him and said, 'Who are you?' And Patrick said to her, 'You and I, we were the shooters! Don't you remember me, Maureen?' And she looked up at him and said, 'Patrick?!' and she started to cry and she stood up and he hugged and kissed her and she put her head on his shoulder and just cried and said, 'What a guy you turned out to be!'"

On Wednesday, January 20, 1993, Maureen's body finally gave out after years of abusing booze and cigarettes, and falling off second-story walkways. Though she had been in and out of hospitals for several months, she died upstairs in her room above the tavern. O'Neill said that a friend in social services had told him that Maureen had been only 52 years old when she died. Other close friends of hers confirmed that.

A closed-casket wake for Kavanaugh was held the following Sunday at Bermingham Funeral Home in Wharton. While Maddie was taking care of the arrangements there, an unexpected drama was playing out back at the tavern. Brenda Foley decided it was time to move in. O'Neill was tending bar at the time.

"While Maureen was being laid out at the funeral home in Wharton, all of the sudden, a cab pulls up out front," O'Neill said. "Brenda pops out of the cab and barrels into the bar with her suitcases. I said, 'What are you doing?' And she said, 'I'm moving in!' I said, 'The hell you are.' I hated her, and she hated me. Next thing you know I'm making her a drink and she started to go into the kitchen to get a pizza. I was thinking to myself, 'Maureen and I had our problems, but I'll be damned if this is going to happen when Maureen is being laid out at the funeral home.' I wasn't going to let her move in while Maureen was laying in her coffin over there in Wharton. Uh-uh-uh."

O'Neill continued to try to get the woman to leave the bar, but Brenda insisted on staying.

"She was just going to move in and have a grand old time," O'Neill said. "She told me, 'Don't give me any guff, because you're the first one who's going to leave here.' And I said, 'No, honey, you are.' She threatened to have me fired. Somehow I got a hold of Maddie at the funeral parlor, and Maddie said, 'What the hell is *she* doing there?' And I don't know if I called her a cab or called somebody else. I used to drink a lot then, so I'm not sure what I said, but I think I said something like 'If you don't get out of here, I'm gonna call the cops. And I think they're looking for you anyway.' I do remember that everyone in the bar applauded me for getting her out of there."

Interestingly, O'Neill's threat to call the police may have been much more potent than anyone suspected. Both O'Neill and Maggie O'Hara claimed that Brenda had at one point been in police custody, but had managed to slip from the grasp of the authorities. Sometime before her dramatic attempt to move in with Maddie, O'Neill claims he got a funny, frantic phone call from an old friend.

"Quick! Turn on the TV! Brenda is on *America's Most Wanted*!," this friend said.

Added O'Hara: "She escaped from jail once, I thought. My friend Don said he saw her on *America's Most Wanted*, too. I never cared for her at all. I didn't think she's a very nice person. I don't pass judgement, because I've done a few things in my life that I'm not proud of, but there was something about her that I didn't like."

After Maureen's funeral, Maddie hosted a reception at the tavern. At one point during the evening, Patsy Cline's *Sweet Dreams* was played on the jukebox, and a hush went over the bar. It had been one of Maureen's favorite songs.

Maureen Kavanaugh had been a powerful presence at Maddie's Mine Hill Tavern for 28 years, and now she was gone for good. Or was she? O'Neill started having some odd experiences around the bar when the reception following Maureen's viewing came to a close.

"On the night of Maureen's wake, I put away all of the bottles and cleaned up and I took Maddie up to bed and put her in bed, then I turned out all of the lights downstairs and locked up. Then I left. The next morning, about six hours later, I came back and Maddie was still in bed, so I went upstairs and woke her up got her out of bed.

"When I went back downstairs, there was a bottle of Maureen's favorite booze sitting there on the edge of the bar, with a paper napkin draped over the top of it. Now, I know Maddie didn't go back downstairs during the night, because she was too drunk. If she was alive today she would back me up on this. She swore she didn't do it. Nobody else was in the building after I left there. I can't explain what happened. It was bizarre."

Had Maureen's spirit returned to the place where she had spent more than half her life? O'Neill thinks so.

"There was another barmaid named Debi," O'Neill recounts. "We used to call her 'Little Debbie.' She was cute. Well, she was working one night after Maureen died, and she called me up, crying hysterically. She told me I had to come right away. When I got there, she pointed to this cowbell behind the bar. It had belonged to Maureen, and Debi told me that she was sitting there alone at the bar when the bell began to ring by itself. Debi knew it was Maureen's bell, and she told me, 'I don't care. Maddie can fire me if she wants to, but I'm not staying here alone tonight.' She made me stay."

Debi Alexander was former barmaid O'Neill spoke about, and she confirmed O'Neill's tale of the cowbell: "Chuck remembered that? Holy crap. And you're going to write that in the book?" she asked. "Great. It'll look like 'Debi the big sissy.' 'Oh, let's call Chuck to rescue me!' But the stuff he said was all pretty much true."

Odd occurrences continued, O'Neill said. "I had some other strange things happen when I was there alone. I'd hear some strange noises upstairs, and I'd go upstairs and there would be nobody there. I'd hear a thump and go upstairs to see what it was. I'd be scared. If anybody haunted that place, Maureen did."

Added Alexander, "That place was haunted. I don't care what anybody else says."

Some are skeptical of the ghostly claims, while others openly embrace them.

"I think a lot of that depends on whether you or I believe in ghosts in the first place," said Stephen Burns. "But if anybody could have been a haunting-type person, it would have been that bitch."

After Maureen's passing, a lot of Maddie's old enthusiasm for her work at the tavern started to wane. She tired more easily and began to complain about her health.

"Maureen's death took a lot out of her," said Lew Rothbart.

"It wasn't the same without Maureen," Winters said. "She loved Maureen very much, even though they fought a lot."

"Oh, she told me so many times, on different nights, how tired she was," said another old friend, Ed Hendricks. "She'd just sit there and she'd be beside herself. She'd say, 'Eddie I don't want to go on.' And I would talk to her about Florida. And I'd tell her that once she got down there she'd be happy."

It wasn't long before Maddie began entertaining serious offers on the sale of the tavern. According to Harvey Klein, Maddie had been offered $500,000 for the place during the height of its popularity in the 1970s, but she turned the offer down. Rothbart claims he later offered her about $200,000 for the place himself. Another tavern regular, Jim Clarke, said he, too, made Maddie an offer in the neighborhood of $200,000. Maddie turned down both deals. Both men subsequently opened their own gay bars in Morris County.

To the great sadness of her longtime customers, Maddie advertised her little tavern for sale and began making tentative plans to move in with her sister Jean in Ocala, Florida. Meantime she continued to grieve for her departed companion, often asking her friend Larry Winters to take her to Gates of Heaven cemetery in East Hanover so she could pay her respects.

"You wouldn't believe, after Maureen died, the Sundays she'd call me up and say, 'Are you going to take me down to Gates of Heaven?' At the time, Harvey Klein was working at the bar at the Marriott on a Sunday, so I'd take her down to the cemetery and afterwards we'd go up there and have a drink with Harvey.

"Sometimes I'd have to half-carry her up to the grave stone. The one time I got her up there, I said to her, 'God, I'm gonna have to dig a hole for you,' because she was so out of breath. We'd water the plants and then afterward we'd go over to Harvey's. The tears would flow. She'd say, 'I should have been nicer to her. I should have done this. I should have done that.' What could I say to the poor woman after the fact?"

In 1994 Maddie found a buyer: Robert Spagna, a retired homebuilder who had operated the Martha Washington Restaurant in Blairstown with his wife, Barbara.

"Maddie had the place for sale for several years, and every time it came close to closing and she had a buyer, it didn't work out," Barbara Spagna said. "The reason was the parking lot didn't have clear title. So everybody backed out. I don't remember how old she was when she sold it to me, but she was definitely ready to get out. She just couldn't handle it anymore, especially when Maureen was gone."

Barbara had actually been friendly with Maddie as early as the 1960s, when they would run into each other at Circle Lanes, a bowling alley in Ledgewood: "She was a lovely person. I knew her husband, too. And he was very nice, too."

Eventually the Spagnas resolved the issue of the disputed title to the parking lot and began inching forward on a deal with Maddie.

"We had been running the Martha Washington for seven years and then retired," Spagna said. "We did very well there. It was population of 5,000 people, and we had a captive audience. We always talked about buying another place. My husband said he would never buy another place unless it was in Morris County. We lived in Morristown. So when I saw the advertisement for Maddie's, I said, 'Let's go look at it.' Then I found out it was this place and I told my husband that I knew Maddie."

By October, 1994 the deal was in place, and the Spagnas agreed to pay either $150,000 or $157,500 for the property (strangely, the monetary figures on the deed are contradictory). After 33 years behind the bar at Maddie's Mine Hill Tavern, 69-year-old Madeline Bellini was finally ready to retire.

"One of the funny things was, the sale was postponed about six times, so we had about six closing parties," Lew Rothbart said. "The final closing party was like the end of a week's celebration. Because every night they were supposed to close and they didn't, and they didn't, and they didn't. Then finally the closing happened. And she left."

On October 13th, Maddie signed the deed over to the Spagnas, but continued to occupy the tavern for another ten days or so. On Saturday the 24th she had her Farewell Party, and the bar was packed with old friends dating back to the 1960s. State ordinances prohibited the free distribution of alcohol, so Maddie sold drinks for ten cents each. Somewhere, Sadie Amato was smiling.

"The mood at the party was good," Rothbart said. "People were happy for Maddie. She was going and people were happy. The booze flowed like water."

"I said a few words, some kind of tribute to her," O'Neill said. "I said that if it wasn't for Maddie's, none of the people in this room would have met, and now you have friendships and bonds that will last a lifetime."

Very true. Of the dozens of people interviewed for this book, many said they had made friendships at Maddie's that endure to this day. Ev had a typical story. She and her companion, Marge, met Randy Sonner at the bar in the mid-1980s, and though he was a generation younger than the two ladies were, the three became fast friends.

"I said to Marge, 'Look at that nice looking dude standing over there by the jukebox. I gotta get him over here with the crowd,'" Ev said. "So I walked over there and I think I asked him what his name was. Maybe I was half in the bag by then. I said, 'Come on, join us. We're over by the bar.' So he did. He came over and that's how I met Randy and from that time on we've been friends."

During the party, Maddie gave away dozens of little bar items. The sign that reads, "This is it, M.H.T." went to Larry Winters. An autographed pool cue went to Ed Hendricks. A couple of wobbly bar stools went to Molly Chapel. A signed neon bulletin board went to O'Neill. A window curtain dating back to the Sadie's era went to a regular patron named Liz Howatt. Stephen Burns got a light fixture that had hung over the pool table. Rothbart received a number of items that were to be used in his gay bar, The Yacht Club, which he opened in October of 1984 in Jefferson Township. That nightclub would now remain the only gay bar in Morris County.

It says something powerful about the great affection for which bar patrons held Maddie's Mine Hill Tavern that today, almost ten years after the tavern's closing, most still hold and value these little souvenirs.

The morning after the big farewell party, O'Neill returned to the tavern to help Maddie move out.

"The next day there were only a few bottles of booze left," O'Neill said. "I went in there to say goodbye to her and close up. When we walked out of the bar, she couldn't close the door. She said, 'You close it.' And I said, 'No, Maddie, you close it.' But she couldn't do it. So I shut the door and gave her the key and I walked over to the car with her. She said, 'I don't think I'll ever see you again.' And I said, 'No, I'll see you again.' I hugged her and I cried so badly. She was a great lady."

Arriving in Florida, Maddie moved in with her sister Jean, in Jean's doublewide trailer. Friends like Stephen Burns, a Florida resident for part of the year, visited her and said she loved living there. Always a heavy drinker, Maddie no longer bore the responsibility of operating a business, so she drank even more than usual.

Meanwhile, back in Mine Hill, the Spagnas undertook a massive renovation of the Mine Hill Tavern. Photographs of the tavern taken just prior to the Spagnas' purchase show a property in serious need of repair. Maddie, say many of her friends, simply refused to put any money into the place, so for 33 years it had been allowed to slowly sag and rot. The Spagnas spent at least $100,000 renovating the place.

"You have to understand there was nothing here," Barbara Spagna said. "There was no restaurant equipment. We had to do the whole commercial kitchen. Everything was totally rebuilt. We poured concrete floors. It was basically a dirt floor with boards laid over it before that."

Spagna said the property was raised twelve inches, essentially gutted and reinforced. A commercial kitchen was placed upstairs in Maddie's old bedroom. Perhaps appropriately, a second bar, dubbed "Dugan's Pub," was installed in the second floor area that had once been Maureen's bedroom. An upscale dining room—walled off in two sections—replaced the bar area at the main entrance, but the Spagnas maintained a smaller bar on the southern end of the former Maddie's bar area, where the pool table had been located.

With an eye to history, the couple decided to rename the property "Cornelius House," in honor of Thomas Cornelius, who had owned the land when James Cox built his hotel there.

"When we started cleaning out the place, everything we put out for the garbage, somebody took as a memento," Barbara said with a laugh. "Nothing made it to the garbage man. A lot of it went up to that place in Jefferson, The Yacht Club. We even had a grand opening sign, 'Grand Opening April 15' out front. We paid a lot of money to have it made. They stole that, too. They took the bar stools that we put out in the garbage, everything."

During renovations, the Spagnas uncovered a beautifully preserved folk art painting of the USS Maine on a wainscot wall under decades of paneling and wallpaper. It was a stunning surprise for the couple and for the Mine Hill community. Like a traveler through time, the painting had re-emerged nearly 100 years after DM Spencer had painted it in 1899. It was during the time when Annie and Richard Barrett—the former Dover beef house operators—owned the property that Spencer first conceived his tableau. The Spagnas immediately had the painting cleaned, photographed and placed in storage.

"They were pulling the wall down behind the bar and they came across [the painting] behind the wall," Barbara said. "I wasn't there. It was my son and Bob. When they showed me a couple of days later, I didn't think too much of it, until they got the whole thing uncovered. It was covered in wallpaper and everything."

208

The discovery of the painting resulted in an intense bout of research into the background of the artist, which to date has failed to provide in any information on the mysterious D.M. Spencer. Spencer had reportedly been from Brooklyn, NY, so calls were made to the Brooklyn Historical Society, the Brooklyn Arts Council, and the Brooklyn Collection at the Brooklyn Public Library, as well as several other New Jersey and New York-based historical and art societies and the Folk Art Society of America. None of these organizations could shed any light at all on the life and work of the artist. Spencer did complete at least one other painting during the same period he immortalized the USS Maine on the wall of the Mine Hill Tavern, however. A local family owns a smaller work, painted on tin, that Spencer reportedly completed at the old Bassett Dairy Farm, which once was located just down Randolph Avenue from the current Cornelius House property.

While intrigued by the painting, the Spagnas were left scratching their heads about what, exactly, they should do with it.

Briefly, the couple considered utilizing the painting as part of the decor of the restaurant, but the style of the work clashed with the Spagna's planned concept for a more elegant decorating scheme. Then they mulled over the idea of mounting the painting upstairs in their new Dugan's Pub, which has a more casual, relaxed atmosphere. That too was vetoed when it became impossible to find a wall that could accommodate the enormous seven-by-nine foot painting.

Ironically, during the Maddie's era, bar lore had it that a certain iron post located inside the bar was supposed to be filled with hundreds of coins dating back to the stagecoach era. Almost everyone who spent any amount of time at the bar had heard about the treasure-filled support post. Maddie took the stories seriously enough to have asked her nephew Butch to remove the post in order to retrieve the treasure.

The support post turned out to be empty, but there was indeed a treasure hidden within the walls of the Mine Hill Tavern. Sotheby's auction house conservatively estimated the value of the USS Maine painting at $10,000 to $15,000.

"Sotheby's would be very pleased to offer this piece in our January 2003 Important Americana sale, which contains a number of items that have already generated considerable interest from museum representatives, collectors and dealers," Nancy Druckerman, Senior Vice President of the Sotheby's American Folk Art Department wrote to Barbara Spagna in September, 2002. "We believe your piece would greatly benefit from, and contribute to, the enthusiasm surrounding the sale."

Spagna opted not to have Sotheby's auction the painting off, however, due largely to the enormous cost of having the heavy, wooden painting shipped into New York City. Instead, the painting remains in the garage of Barbara Spagna's Morristown home. She's currently looking for a buyer.

When renovations to the property were complete, the Spagnas hosted a luncheon for the Ferromonte Historical Society of Mine Hill, and Robert Spagna discussed the painting and the overall historical interest of the property at length.

Over the past 126 years, the Mine Hill Tavern had played host to illiterate Irish miners and at least one accused rapist/murderer. It was rumored to have been a speakeasy and a house of ill repute. John Bone probably died there and Maureen Kavanaugh certainly did. Elizabeth Ellis drowned in the Morris Canal while owning the property. Russell Glass drowned in Cozy Lake while owning it. It had been sold in sheriff's auction, was purchased by an heiress and for decades it was the closest thing to a gay honkytonk that New Jersey had ever produced. Jim Gainer rolled off the second floor walkway during an act of love in the 1930s. Lord knows how many people had used the outhouses, rest rooms and parking lot for similar endeavors in the 1960s, 70s, 80s and 90s.

Now, suddenly the old Mine Hill Tavern was going respectable.

CHAPTER ELEVEN

Afterward

On January 21, 1995, the horrible news spread like a shockwave amongst Northern New Jersey's gay community: Madeline Bellini had been killed in a car accident the previous day, almost exactly three months since her Farewell Party and two years to the day since Maureen's death.

In typical Maddie fashion, she, Winters and her sister Jean had just come out of a bar when the accident occurred. In the short time she had lived in the Ocala area, Maddie had befriended a couple who had owned a local tavern and had taken them under her wing.

"There was a bar that was five or six miles from where they were living," Winters said. "It was called the Silver Fox. That's where they frequented. Maddie got close to the young people that owned the place. She was teaching them how to run the place because they'd just bought it."

According to the police report, the crash occurred at 5:50 p.m. on January 20th as Maddie's car was crossing Route 441 to go into the parking lot of Luigi's restaurant there. Maddie was the only fatality. She was the only one who had not been wearing her safety belt.

"Madeline was in my arms, lying across me," Larry Winters says of the moment of her demise. "I was dazed and I could feel myself getting weak. I was shaking her and shaking her. Then somebody knocked on the window and said, 'Your friend is gone.' I just held onto her. Everything hit on my side. I had four broken ribs. Of course I didn't feel anything at the time. Then they started cutting us out of the car. Someone said, 'Don't look at her. Don't look.' But I just grabbed her and looked at her in the face. Her eyes were half-open. I said to her, "Madeline, I love ya. I'll keep the faith.' And I always have.

"Just like that. That was it."

Rescue workers cut Winters and Jean Sharp out of the car and placed the two surviving passengers in a grassy area on the side of the road to determine if there were any broken bones or other serious injuries. Both had been banged up pretty badly and would require weeks of recovery time.

"Our legs were swollen," Winters said. "We both slept in straight chairs for four weeks because we couldn't lie down. My teeth were all loosened. But we survived it."

Members of Maddie's family and lifelong friends like Joey Campisi (Maddie's godchild and sometime bartender) urged Larry and Jean to return to New Jersey for the funeral, but it just wasn't possible.

"We couldn't come out because we were all beaten up. I didn't have to, because I held her in my arms and she was within me. She's part of me. She's in my laughter and in my tears."

When they were sufficiently recovered, Jean and Larry went into Maddie's room to sort through her things. They found literally hundreds of photographs stacked up in boxes and suitcases, a pictorial record of one woman's life.

"There were valises full of pictures," Winters said. "Jeanie told me I could have what I wanted, and I picked out certain ones to take home with me. Several months later Jeanie called from Florida. She said, 'I feel so bad. I had a junk man come and take everything. I should have mailed all this stuff to you.' The photos that I didn't take were disposed of. I just took what I thought our people would enjoy to have."

Many of the photographs featured in this book are from Winters' collection and are published with his blessing. Since "Larry Winters" is a pseudonym, these photos are uncredited.

Maddie, at least on the surface, had lived a thrifty life. She didn't buy lavish clothes or jewelry or go on exotic vacations. Many bar regulars speculated that she must have died fairly wealthy, assuming she had reaped huge profits from the bar's boom time of the 1970s and 80s and spent little of it. There was also the fact that the proceeds from the sale of Maddie's Mine Hill Tavern had not yet been used to purchase new property, so it must have been largely untouched.

Winters disputes this, however.

"She had bills, debts, credit cards," Winters said. "Jeanie and I went through them all. In the later years the business wasn't as good, and she had liability insurance and all that."

After her debts were paid, the remainder of her estate went to a few friends and family members. Vickie Campisi, a friend who had known Maddie at least since the 1940s, when both worked at the MacGregor clothing company in Dover, was the executrix. She received the bulk of Maddie's estate. Four members of the Campisi family each were bequeathed $1,000. Joe Campisi, Jr. was bequeathed $25,000. Jeanie, $10,000. Butch, $5,000.

"Maddie was sorry—terribly sorry—she had sold her place," Winters said of Maddie's state of mind during the last weeks of her life. "It was her home."

Still, Maddie had been looking to the future. Winters said she had her eye on a little piece of property in central Ocala that she thought would make a cute little tavern.

"It was an old building," Winters said. "She said, 'I gotta get Chuckie [O'Neill] down here. You tell Chuckie he's gotta come down here 'cause I'm gonna open that place up as a bar. It's just a small place, but it's good enough. And I'll take care of Chuckie. You tell him that.'"

Back in New Jersey, shock turned to grief as crowds flocked to the Bermingham Funeral Home in Wharton to pay their last respects. Among the flowers and photographs that decorated the viewing room, Maddie lay, dressed in a tasteful pastel suit, a rosary draped in her hands. It was a stark contrast to the Maddie most of her tavern's regulars knew in life, when she typically could be found in a sweatshirt with the front stained from her most recent meal.

At the funeral services, many broke down sobbing when her casket was brought to the front of St. Mary's Church in Wharton, just a mile or two from her old tavern. A half-dozen friends eulogized Maddie, including Maggie O'Hara.

It was a bitter cold day when she was laid to rest with Maureen at Gates of Heaven Cemetery. Her gravestone reads:

MAUREEN M.
KAVANAUGH
JAN 20 1993
SWEET DREAMS
MADELINE
BELLINI
JAN 20 1995

Frank Bellini had been buried in the same cemetery, but Maddie had chosen to be buried with Maureen. In the end, there was no more ambiguity about their love life. Two years after death had come between them, the two women were reunited.

Four months after Maddie's death, on April 15, 1995, the Spagnas reopened the Mine Hill Tavern as the Cornelius House restaurant. Ironically, Sadie Amato had died on that same date precisely 28 years earlier.

"A lot of Maddie's customers became our customers," Spagna said. Knowing how closely many of Maddie's customers held the place in their hearts, Robert and Barbara encouraged them to stop by. Though the interior of the property was vastly different from the Maddie's days, the exterior appeared largely unchanged but for a fresh coat of beige paint and some elegant new signage.

Inside, sharp-eyed customers noticed that a few things hadn't changed. The tiny, square pedestal tables used at Maddie's had been recycled for Cornelius House. The exposed pipes that ran the length of the ceiling of the former bar area's western wall remained, as did an old radiator under one of the windows overlooking Randolph Ave. Befitting the gender-bending nature of the property's past, the rest rooms were reversed under the Spagna's ownership. What had been the men's room of Maddie's became the ladies' room of Cornelius House and vice versa.

Typically, light jazz or classical music was played on the restaurant's P.A. system, but when a former Maddie's regular entered the place, Bob would switch the music to Patsy Cline. Encouraged to come back again and again, Winters said, there would often be two or three gay couples sitting at the little Cornelius House bar, all holdovers from the Maddie's era.

At the Yacht Club in Jefferson Township—now the only gay bar in Morris County—Lewis Rothbart set aside one of the side bar rooms for a tribute to his old friend Madeline Bellini. The place was filled with Maddie's memorabilia, including her old jukebox. Rothbart even hired one of Maddie's barmaid's to work the room. Photographs of Maddie and Maureen dotted the walls. The "Maddie's Mine Hill Tavern" sign that used to hang on the front of the building went up on the wall of the little bar area.

"After Maddie died, we did a six month tribute to her," Rothbart said. "When Maddie died it was a big loss. She was a personal friend. We had a lot of good times in her place. She was part of the gay history of Morris County, part of the gay history of New Jersey."

Though she had given away much Mine Hill Tavern memorabilia in the months prior to her death, Maddie had planned to auction off what she believed to be the most important relic of the tavern—an old bar stool that had sat behind the bar of the tavern since, by her estimates, at least the 1930s. Sadie Amato had left it to her. The auction didn't occur in her lifetime, but in 1995 the stool ended up in the hands of Stephen Burns, who with Rothbart decided to move forward with Maddie's wishes to sell the item for charity.

Advertisements for the barstool sale appeared in local gay publications like *PM*.

"BEFORE STONEWALL THERE WAS MADDIES," the headline of one of the ads reads, before encapsulating the essential details of Maddie's life—owner of the tavern for 33 years, retired to Florida, tragically killed in an automobile accident.

"Before she closed her business she was in the process of 'cleaning house' and stated that she would auction off her 'over 70 year old' barstool. Well, she never got around to holding this acution [sic]. So now, 'BEFORE STONEWALL, THERE WAS MADDIES" has come into possession of said barstool and will hold a raffle to benefit THE ERIC JOHNSON HOUSE, Morristown, New Jersey."

The mission of Eric Johnson House is to provide assistance and permanent housing for those living with HIV/AIDS. The barstool raffle was a nice idea that never happened. For some reason the event never got off the ground. Maddie's old barstool now sits in Burns' garage in Succasunna.

Meanwhile business remained brisk at Cornelius House. Bob and Barbara and their two sons enjoyed running the place as much as Maddie and Maureen had. Bob, described as a warm, elegant man, handled the "upstairs" duties at the restaurant—accounting, billing, personnel, etc.—while Barbara managed the restaurant itself and did the cooking.

"We had a good time," Barbara said. "We made a lot of nice friends there."

Sadly, the couple's happiness would be shattered about two and a half years after purchasing the Mine Hill Tavern, when Bob was diagnosed with multiple myloma, a form of cancer. He then underwent a series of treatments that severely compromised his immune system. Barbara said that despite his discomfort, Bob remained upbeat and cheerful about his prospects. She was surprised to hear, later, of an encounter between Bob and a local man in which Bob betrayed an uncharacteristic pessimism.

Abbie Ebner, who volunteers at what was then Dover General Hospital (it is now a nursing home facility), said he was walking through the hospital lobby in the late 1990s when he encountered Bob, whom he had known from the few times he had dined at Cornelius House.

"I saw him and walked over to say hello," Abbie said. "I said, 'Hi Bob, how are you doing?' And he said, 'I'm dying.'"

Robert Spagna died in August of 1999 at Morristown Memorial Hospital. He was 72.

For a while, Barbara tried to run the place on her own, but it was really too much for one person. "All of the sudden," she said poignantly, "I was doing everything."

On November 5, 2001 she sold the property to Randolph Ave. 181 LLC, a corporate entity created by former New York City restaurant manager Peter Damascus. Damascus, who is in his thirties, moved into the third floor of the building with his wife and baby daughter. Once again, as was so often the case in the property's 133-

year history, the owners of the property lived upstairs while they maintained the business below.

"When the baby's crying, we can just run upstairs," Damascus said when visited at his restaurant in the Spring of 2002.

Damascus did some light renovation—changing the color scheme and some of the furnishings—but the property remained essentially unaltered from the Spagna period. The Morris *Daily Record* reviewed the restaurant on May 10, 2002, and gave it three stars out of four, an "excellent" rating.

"First-rate finely diced tomatoes combined with garlic and a zesty vinaigrette made the complimentary bruschetta memorable, while good Italian bread served with very good olive oil kept us munching while we looked over the quite extensive northern and southern Italian menu: 15 pasta choices and almost two dozen chicken, veal, seafood, steak and vegetarian entrees, plus a few nightly specials," wrote food critic Jean Graham.

Damascus had worked in the New York City restaurant business during the economic boom of the 1990s, and like many in that industry, always dreamed of owning his own place. With rents in Manhattan skyrocketing during the period, Damascus started looking outside the city for a decent property.

"I found Cornelius House on the Internet, and between what you're getting—the property, the liquor license, the building—I thought it was a good deal. I jumped into it," he said during a telephone interview in March of 2003. What he wanted to develop was a New York City-style restaurant, he said, where late diners could get good food in a nice atmosphere. Weekday business in many New York restaurants tends to be brisk, with businesspeople getting off work late and making dates to meet at 7 p.m. or later. Damascus hoped to attract the same kind of upscale crowd.

"When you talk about a New York City-style here in the suburbs, well, I really didn't look into the viability of that as much as maybe I should have," Damascus said. "When you're in the city, you work until 6 or 7 at night, and everyone meets for drinks or dates on a Monday, a Tuesday, a Wednesday. They don't wait until Friday or Saturday night to come in and eat. That was the part I did not realize. Everyone out here, and probably at all suburban areas, goes out and spends money mainly on Friday and Saturday nights. There's no real late dining out that much. You don't find big parties coming in at 9 p.m. In the city people keep on eating till 11 o'clock at night. You start to see, in the suburbs, how TV and sports events really effects your business. In January and February we had the winter Olympics and we had 21 days of an empty restaurant."

Compounding his problem was the recession that followed the terrorist attacks of September 11, Damascus said. He started shopping around for restaurant properties during a boom period, and found himself opening a property during a bust.

"We went under contract to buy the place in July of 2001. The closing wasn't until November, 2001, after 9/11. So after all that money was flowing around for all those years, terrorism strikes and everyone's a little tighter with their pocketbooks. Recession has hit. So I'm starting a restaurant in the New York-style in that environment. And that was it."

At this writing, Cornelius House is once again on the market. Despite his difficulties keeping the restaurant profitable, Damascus says the operation of the property was a learning experience he needed to have.

"It's heart-wrenching," he said. "I'm not going to sell because I made $5 million in one year. But every restaurant person has to go through it, and learn day-in and day-out what the customer wants."

Given the sometimes-unusual history of the place, one has to wonder, did Peter or his family ever experience anything out of the ordinary? Did maybe Maureen Kavanaugh stop by for a visit?

"Barbara [Spagna]'s daughter-in-law used to worked here, and she used to tease me: 'When you're closing up, what do you hear here?' And then my imagination would really go, because for a good part of the time I'd be alone at night. They would always say there was something, but I never heard anything move or shake. I have a security system, and only once did it go off for no reason in the one and a half years that I've had it. So I don't think there's anything going on. But I have to say, on the night we shut everything down, there was an eerie silence. After a year and a half of running all of the refrigeration units, the silence was suddenly deafening."

In November of 2002, Damascus closed Cornelius House. In March of 2003 he was commuting into New York daily to work in a restaurant above Grand Central Station.

In 2000, Lewis Rothbart's Yacht Club closed its doors, and the building was demolished in 2002. Another tenuous tie to the Maddie's era had faded away. But times were changing. Many gay people no longer felt stigmatized by their sexuality. TV programs like *Will & Grace* and *Queer As Folk* were high-profile gay-themed hits. Entertainers like k.d. lang, Melissa Etheridge, Elton John, George Michael, Nathan Lane and Rupert Everett are decidedly mainstream. High schools have gay and lesbian support groups. Twentisomethings can find each other through Internet dating services and chat boards. The gay bar is no longer the center of gay life that it once was. People simply have other options.

One enormously visible indication of the mainstreaming of homosexuality is the location of Morris County's newest (and only) gay bar. Opened in 1996, Connexions nightclub is situated in the center of Boonton, at the 100-year-old train station—as much a local institution as city hall or the public library—by which hundreds of commuters pass daily on their way to and from Hoboken and New York City.

Former Maddie's regulars Jim Clarke and Ray Sonderfan run the place. A photo of Maddie and Maureen even adorns the bar. Downstairs in a back room is a photo montage tribute to Maddie's. Here, appropriately, is the most recent resting-place of the huge plywood "Maddie's Mine Hill Tavern" sign that had once graced the front of the Mine Hill Tavern and then hung on an inside wall at the Yacht Club. Stop in at the bar on any Sunday evening and you're likely to run into five or six old Maddie's customers mixed in with younger generations of gay men and women.

Sonderfan, about thirty at the time this book was being researched, remembered walking into Maddie's at the tender age of 17.

"The first time I met Maureen she said, 'Get out! We don't serve your kind here!'" Ray says with a laugh. "She either thought I was underage—which I was—or straight. Then she whipped my butt playing pool and fell in love with me. As long as I didn't drink there, and abided by her rules and Maddie's rules, she was fine with me and I could stay."

For a while, in a case of perfect symmetry, Lew Rothbart could be found working behind the bar at Connexions, continuing his quarter-century association with gay bars in Morris County. Then, in 2003, in yet another demonstration of the "mainstreaming" of gay culture, Rothbart became manager of the influential New Jersey State Licensed Beverage Association and took an office in the state capital. When he first began his career as an openly gay man in 1978, a career move like that would have been almost unthinkable.

As these words are being keyed in, Cornelius House is dark, though the tables inside remain covered in white linen, the napkins neatly folded, the silverware and glassware in place as if the restaurant had just been closed last night, rather than six months ago.

Throughout Northern New Jersey, however, there are small reminders of the people that made their mark on the little property on the corner of Randolph and West Randolph Avenues in Mine Hill. You just have to be willing to look around a little. If you were to drive around the tightly clustered little neighborhoods just off Maine Street in the center of Wharton, for example, you might come upon a once-grand Second Empire building with a mansard roof and two-story porch on Second Street. Now apartments, this vinyl-sided building with the satellite dish protruding from the front was once the Wharton Hotel, likely the same property where once worked "Grandmother" Elizabeth Ellis, the world's oldest living bartender, before her demise. Head out to the Presbyterian Cemetery in Rockaway and you can find Elizabeth's last resting place, and nearby are former Mine Hill Hotel owners James and Elizabeth Matthews, Elizabeth's daughter and son-in-law.

Take a drive through Dover and you're likely to encounter an intersection that exists largely because the Glass family gave up their rights to a piece of property in the 1930s when settling the Augusta Glass estate. Drive past Cornelius House en route to Canfield Ave. and you'll to pass the residence of one of Art Glass's descendants, who for over fifty years has watched as the little tavern on the corner of Randolph and West Randolph changed with the times.

If you happen to be driving that route after midnight, pause at the intersection of Canfield and West Randolph and take a careful look around. You just might see the ghost of John Smith, or the woman in white.

Turn left at that intersection and within a minute or so you'll see a signpost on the side of the road. It marks the spot where the Dickerson Mine once churned out thousands of pounds of iron ore every year. How many miners stopped at the tavern at the Mine Hill Hotel for a drink on the way home from a hazardous day of work, dozens of feet below ground? We'll probably never know.

Swing back toward Randolph Ave. proper, drive on past Cornelius House and pause at the front of the little saltbox Bridget Smith House, clearly marked by a plaque designating it a historic landmark. Give a passing thought to old Ida McConnell, who witnessed the horror of influenza in 1918, later chased her husband out of the Mine Hill Hotel's tavern, and lived into her 104th year.

Two or three houses down the road is Joann's Bar, where the funny Asian-American woman behind the bar will tell you that no, she did *not* shoot her husband and, yes, she was very good friends with Madeline Bellini. And have you tried the nachos?

Go have a drink at the At the Hop tavern in Dover. Hanging on the wall of that colorful watering hole is a toilet seat. Lift the lid and you'll see a photo of the person who's on the bad list that month. The toilet seat is from the ladies' room of Maddie's Mine Hill Tavern. If that toilet seat could talk, you wouldn't want to hear what it had to say.

Drop by the Gold Coin Chinese restaurant in Dover. There, on any given day, you might catch Harvey Klein sitting at the bar, having a cocktail. Nudge him a little and he'll tell you about his exploits in Hollywood and on Broadway. Nudge him again and he'll tell you all about blowsy old Hazel Lapadula. Or he may tell you to please stop with the nudging already.

Head out to the main drag in Rockaway some night and check out a few of the local drinking establishments. You just might run into an old-timer who knew Madeline Bellini about as well as anybody ever knew her. He'll tell you all you need to know about the old Mine Hill Tavern. He might even personally introduce you to the old dame who once ran the joint.

"I could be at a bar, talking to some fella, laughing and having a good time, and I'll look over my shoulder and there they'll be," he'll say, "Maddie and Maureen, sitting there at the bar."

When asked to describe Maddie's Mine Hill Tavern for someone who had never been there, several regulars referred to it as a "neighborhood bar," but if that's true, the Maddie's neighborhood stretched far beyond the boundaries of Randolph Avenue in Mine Hill.

It seems fitting to sum up the widespread affection people felt for the tavern and its proprietor with a telling anecdote by Mine Hill Police Chief Richard Lansing. During his tenure as chief, Lansing and a Mine Hill sergeant drove their patrol car down to Trenton to get new license plates for the vehicle, a distance of seventy miles.

"We're on a street in Trenton, and a guy standing on the corner saw the Mine Hill Police emblem on the car," Lansing said. "And this guy shouts to us.

"'Hey, Mine Hill!,' he says, 'Tell Maddie I said hello!'"

AUTHOR'S NOTES AND ACKNOWLEDGEMENTS

Mine Hill, NJ is not Provincetown, Mass. or New Hope, Penn. It is not an artist community that openly celebrates alternative lifestyles. During the 30 years or so that the Mine Hill Tavern functioned as a gay bar, there was a certain amount of tension in the community over the scores of gay out-of-towners that flocked to the little village to visit the tavern. Much of this tension, it should be said, was due to the traffic congestion and parking problems caused during the tavern's peak of popularity in the 1970s and 80s.

At least some of that tension, though, was undoubtedly due to a discomfort with homosexuality. There may have been more fights at Joann's, and more openly salacious behavior at the Rest-a-Bit strip club on Route 46 in town, but the Mine Hill Tavern was singled out by a few of the more conservative elements of the community for special scorn.

On the other hand, Mine Hill, NJ is also not Laramie, Wyoming, where in 1998 local intolerance displayed itself so tragically when a young man was beaten and tied to a fence to die simply because he was gay. Indeed, as early as the 1930s, a pair of women who most assumed were lesbian lived together peacefully in Mine Hill without incident. Abbie Ebner fondly remembered these two ladies:

"We had neighbors that many people in the neighborhood thought were probably gay," Abbie said during the course of my first conversation with him. "They were two women, brilliant women. Alice Scudder was probably the brightest woman I've ever known in the course of my life. Her companion was Catherine Callen. They lived there from 1932 until Alice died in 1995 or thereabouts. Then Catherine died about a year or two later. They were gems."

They also bought young Abbie his first bicycle.

So no, Mine Hill, NJ was not Laramie, Wyoming. If there were a few locals who were uncomfortable with the sexual orientation of the patrons of Maddie's Mine Hill Tavern, most decided to live and let live. And that, truly, says something pretty remarkable about this tiny village halfway between Manhattan and the Pennsylvania border which was founded largely on the backs of hardscrabble working men

223

and for which the biggest event each summer is the annual firemen's carnival.

I myself was never a "regular" at the Mine Hill Tavern. At most, I stopped by once or twice a month during the last two years of Madeline Bellini's ownership. Maureen Kavanaugh was behind the bar the first time I walked into the bar, sometime in early 1992. My companion, Randall Sonner (who is also quoted in this book) had already been stopping by the place for five or six years by that time, and he warned me that the interior of the bar, in his words, "looks like somebody's basement." I was only five years out of college, and had spent more than my fair share of time drinking cheap beer in dank basement bars of fraternity houses, so Randy's comment had no real effect on me.

We walked in and I took a seat on a wobbly bar stool and ordered a glass of wine. When Maureen brought it over, the wine glass had an inscription on it; something like, "Congratulations Kevin and Edna, May 12th, 1989." It was obviously a keepsake from someone's wedding.

The quality of the drinks themselves was often as erratic as the glassware. If Maureen was tending bar and she liked you, she'd make the drinks the way she drank them herself—so strong they could peel wallpaper from drywall. Because I was always polite to her, she often served me cocktails that were almost undrinkable—screwdrivers that had only the faintest blush of orange juice in them, rum and cokes with just a thimbleful of Coca-Cola. But Maureen was so moody that sometimes you were better off just trying to sip the drink as-is rather than ask for another. I once managed to swallow a few gulps of one blisteringly strong cocktail before I worked up the courage to say, "Thanks, Maureen, but could you make the next one a little bit weaker?"

She eyed me contemptuously and sneered, "I *don't make* strong drinks!"

Obviously as I worked on this project I was as careful to be as accurate in all details as possible. However, much of my research into the early days of the Mine Hill Tavern was based on local newspaper accounts of the day, which sometimes contained incomplete or contradictory information. Newspaper writing of the 1800s was far different from that of the twentieth and twenty-first centuries, and readers used to modern reporting might find newspaper stories of an earlier era dense and cumbersome, though charming in their own way. I tried for the sake of clarity and pithiness to distill some of this coverage to its essence, while at the same time I attempted to capture the old world style and charm of these old accounts.

In the case of the murder of Mary Ann Moore, a great deal of the testimony from the trial of her husband came from the *Jerseyman* newspaper coverage. This coverage was in some ways comprehensive (there was an account of the jury selection, what appears to be detailed notes on each witness's testimonies, and a long rundown of the attorneys summations and the judge's closing comments) and in some ways incomplete (there was little context to the coverage, and few direct quotes).

Typical of the *Jerseyman*'s coverage of the trial was their accounting of Dr. Thomas Crittenden's testimony, which reads very much like reporter's notes: "Dr. Thos. Crittenden sworn: Am a practising physician at Dover; have practised 25 years; made a post mortem examination of body of Mary Ann Moore on Saturday, Nov. 30, assisted by Dr. Condict, at Irishtown; body was of frail make, about 35 or 40 years old…"

From these detailed accountings, I sometimes paraphrased the testimony and sometimes cleaned up the language and punctuation and placed phrases in direct quotes. In the case of Bridget Grady, for example, her testimony—if lifted directly from the *Jerseyman*—reads as follows:

"Knows Moore and knew his wife; about a month before Mrs. Moore's death I saw David kick her and break a fiddle over her head; she was down on the ground and he kicked her in the side of the stomach; Mrs. Lucas and myself saw him do this; we didn't dare go near her to assist her; I helped wash the body after death, saw old black and blue marks on her, and she often deserved beating too; I don't like to be too hard on him."

In chapter three I distilled Grady's comments and quoted her directly where I thought appropriate. Here's how her testimony appears in that chapter:

"Bridget Grady testified that about a month before Mary Ann's death, she had seen Moore kick her in the side and stomach and break a fiddle over her head. 'We didn't dare go near her to assist her,' she said. 'I helped wash the body after her death, saw old black and blue marks on her, and she often deserved beating, too. I don't like to be too hard on him.'"

I did less of this type of distillation, and made fewer changes to punctuation and quotation in the later trial accounts of the Smith and Gallagher murders, when the newspaper coverage was more contemporary in its approach.

In several cases, individuals asked that their identities be protected, so I changed their names for the purposes of this book. When the names of these same individuals appeared in quotations, I again substituted the real names for the pseudonyms. Beyond the alterations of individual names, however, the stories and quotations in this book are essentially as they were recounted to me. This point was footnoted within the text of the book itself, but it perhaps bears repeating to avoid confusion.

I started out my research on this book imagining I would produce a slim little volume dealing with the purely cultural and sociological aspects of Maddie's Mine Hill Tavern, specifically, the strange evolution of a gay bar in the center of a rural, blue collar community. But when I began looking into the property's long history, the book began to take on a life of its own. It seemed as if the more I dug into the tavern's past, the more odd, fascinating tales I came up with in connection the place. Before long, the Mine Hill Tavern had become a kind of glorious obsession with me.

Along the way to the book's completion I was aided by many individuals who gave generously of their time, their energies and their points of view. About halfway through the course of my research, former Ferromonte Historical Society of Mine Hill President Elaine Campoli introduced me to her next-door neighbor, Abbie Ebner. Elaine has a passion for history and she was a great help in accessing individuals and resources that moved my research forward. Abbie and his wife Kitty became close friends during the course of my research, and this book would not have been nearly as complete without

Abbie's assistance. With his wide network of friends who are longtime Mine Hill area residents, Abbie set up one interview after another for me with various senior citizens that were regulars at the tavern during the Art Glass and Sadie Amato periods. I'm terribly grateful to him for his enormous help.

"Stephen Burns," a former Maddie's regular, was similarly helpful in connecting me to individuals who frequented the tavern during the 1970s and 80s, and providing me with photographs, memorabilia and a copy of his videotaped interview with Maddie and tour of the bar, shot just weeks before she sold the tavern and moved to Florida. He took obvious delight in my research and sent me a near-constant stream of names and telephone numbers of folks whom he thought would provide information.

Harvey Klein and "Larry Winters" gave dozens of little insights into the place, and Larry generously allowed me to borrow from his vast collection of Maddie's photographs for this book.

My dear friends Maureen Campbell and Noelle Daidone provided constant support and encouragement as this work was being completed, and enthusiastically read the working drafts of the book as they were completed, providing valuable and constructive comments along the way.

I also wish to acknowledge the assistance of the Morristown Public Library's Local History and Genealogy Department: John Medallis, Chrys Jochem, Cheryl Turkington and Claire Kissel.

Very late in the process of writing this book, I was lucky enough to discover the archives of the Morris County Heritage Commission, overseen by David Mitros. During the three days I spent at his office, pouring over old tavern licenses and pestering him about having multiple copies of made, David was endlessly patient and encouraging.

And of course I'd like to thank my companion, Randy, my parents and my six brothers and sisters for their years of help and support.

ABOUT THE AUTHOR

Award-winning journalist Matt Connor is Senior Editor of *IGWB*, a gaming industry trade magazine, and is Editor of *Indian Gaming Business*, which covers the multi-billion dollar Indian casino industry. Previously, Connor was Managing Editor of the menswear magazine *MR*. Through a bizarre series of events, Connor once found himself stranded in a helicopter with Elizabeth Taylor. He was subsequently hired as an editor by Taylor's friend, the late billionaire publisher Malcolm Forbes. Connor's work has appeared in *Forbes FYI, Men's Style, Unique Homes* and many other publications. A friend of the late singer Rosemary Clooney, Connor contributes regularly to www.rosemaryclooney.com. He resides in N.J. with his companion of twelve years and their four Boston Terriers, Emma, Sammy, Sophie and Harry.

Printed in the United States
16507LVS00004B/64-168

9 781414 003030